KENTUCKY FIGHTING MEN

1861-1945

RICHARD G. STONE, Jr.

THE UNIVERSITY PRESS OF KENTUCKY

Copyright © 1982 by The University Press of Kentucky
Paperback edition 2009

The University Press of Kentucky
Scholarly publisher for the Commonwealth,
serving Bellarmine University, Berea College, Centre
College of Kentucky, Eastern Kentucky University,
The Filson Historical Society, Georgetown College,
Kentucky Historical Society, Kentucky State University,
Morehead State University, Murray State University,
Northern Kentucky University, Transylvania University,
University of Kentucky, University of Louisville,
and Western Kentucky University.
All rights reserved.

Editorial and Sales Offices: The University Press of Kentucky
663 South Limestone Street, Lexington, Kentucky 40508-4008
www.kentuckypress.com

Cataloging-in-Publication Data is available from
the Library of Congress.

ISBN 978-0-8131-9314-4 (pbk: acid-free paper)

This book is printed on acid-free recycled paper meeting
the requirements of the American National Standard
for Permanence in Paper for Printed Library Materials.

Manufactured in the United States of America.

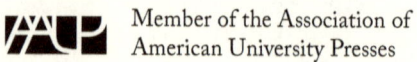

The Kentucky Bicentennial Bookshelf
Sponsored by
KENTUCKY HISTORICAL EVENTS CELEBRATION COMMISSION
KENTUCKY FEDERATION OF WOMEN'S CLUBS
and Contributing Sponsors
AMERICAN FEDERAL SAVINGS & LOAN ASSOCIATION
ARMCO STEEL CORPORATION, ASHLAND WORKS
A. ARNOLD & SON TRANSFER & STORAGE CO., INC. / ASHLAND OIL, INC.
BAILEY MINING COMPANY, BYPRO, KENTUCKY / BEGLEY DRUG COMPANY
J. WINSTON COLEMAN, JR. / CONVENIENT INDUSTRIES OF AMERICA, INC.
IN MEMORY OF MR. AND MRS. J. SHERMAN COOPER BY THEIR CHILDREN
CORNING GLASS WORKS FOUNDATION / MRS. CLORA CORRELL
THE COURIER-JOURNAL AND THE LOUISVILLE TIMES
COVINGTON TRUST & BANKING COMPANY
MR. AND MRS. GEORGE P. CROUNSE / GEORGE E. EVANS, JR.
FARMERS BANK & CAPITAL TRUST COMPANY / FISHER-PRICE TOYS, MURRAY
MARY PAULINE FOX, M.D., IN HONOR OF CHLOE GIFFORD
MARY A. HALL, M.D., IN HONOR OF PAT LEE
JANICE HALL & MARY ANN FAULKNER
OSCAR HORNSBY, INC. / OFFICE PRODUCTS DIVISION IBM CORPORATION
JERRY'S RESTAURANTS / ROBERT B. JEWELL
LEE S. JONES / KENTUCKIANA GIRL SCOUT COUNCIL
KENTUCKY BANKERS ASSOCIATION / KENTUCKY COAL ASSOCIATION, INC.
THE KENTUCKY JOCKEY CLUB, INC. / THE LEXINGTON WOMAN'S CLUB
LINCOLN INCOME LIFE INSURANCE COMPANY
LORILLARD A DIVISION OF LOEW'S THEATRES, INC.
METROPOLITAN WOMAN'S CLUB OF LEXINGTON / BETTY HAGGIN MOLLOY
MUTUAL FEDERAL SAVINGS & LOAN ASSOCIATION
NATIONAL INDUSTRIES, INC. / RAND MCNALLY & COMPANY
PHILIP MORRIS, INCORPORATED / MRS. VICTOR SAMS
SHELL OIL COMPANY, LOUISVILLE
SOUTH CENTRAL BELL TELEPHONE COMPANY
SOUTHERN BELLE DAIRY CO., INC.
STANDARD OIL COMPANY (KENTUCKY)
STANDARD PRINTING CO., H. M. KESSLER, PRESIDENT
STATE BANK & TRUST COMPANY, RICHMOND
THOMAS INDUSTRIES INC. / TIP TOP COAL CO., INC.
MARY L. WISS, M.D. / YOUNGER WOMAN'S CLUB OF ST. MATTHEWS

*For Richard G. Stone
and Marye Grove Stone*

Contents

Prologue ix

1 / Proud to Be Alive and a Kentuckian 1

2 / Reaching Abroad (1865–1918) 26

3 / Remember Pearl Harbor! 57

4 / Avengers of Bataan 93

Epilogue 116

Acknowledgments and Sources 119

Index 123

Prologue

*There stood John Bull in martial pomp,
But here stood old Kentucky!*

THE BRITISH would attack at dawn. So ran the familiar folk yarn that improved with age, like Kentucky bourbon. In defense of New Orleans stood only a pitiful rabble of an American army, huddled behind a long, low rampart of mud and cotton bales stretching away from the Mississippi into a mucky cypress swamp. But the invaders took too lightly Old Hickory Jackson—and the hunters of Kentucky. Andrew Jackson felt no dread; he knew what a deadly bead his hardy, freeborn Kentuckians could draw with their graceful long rifles. Why, every Kentuckian there at Chalmette on that eighth of January in 1815 was half-horse and half-alligator! Each man carried a gun, a pack of cards, and a bottle of whiskey. None would waste his precious powder—not until the hated redcoats drew so close that you could see them wink: *And 'twould have done you good, I think, / To see Kentuckians drop 'em / O Kentucky, the hunters of Kentucky.*

Like so much popular mythology, Samuel Woodworth's hoary ditty "The Hunters of Kentucky" surrounds a kernel of truth. About eight hundred sons of the Bluegrass did indeed fight behind the storied parapet at Rodriguez Canal on that long-ago chilly January morning. But the Kentucky contingent was only a small part of Jackson's motley army. The real noteworthiness of Woodworth's doggerel is its reminder to us of the early American military tradition of the citizen-volunteer soldier, a tradition closely associated with Kentucky. The Bluegrass State evoked an image of log blockhouses, war whoops, long rifles, buckskins, and Bowie knives for decades before it conjured up an equally distorted vision of mint juleps, burgoo, damsels in hoopskirts, thoroughbred horses, and stately antebellum brick mansions.

For almost half a century before the Battle of New Orleans thousands of pioneers had found irresistible the urge to settle west of the Alleghenies. "Bust my coonskins, William," says J. I. Corby's fictional version of the scout Simon Kenton. "Yo're a sight fur sore eyes! Whatever brung you out thisaway?" Kenton's old friend from Virginia responds, "Fauquier County's gittin' too small fur us, too." It took the pioneer founders of Kentucky some twenty years of fighting, from 1774 to 1794, to wrest away the Dark and Bloody Ground from its original redskinned possessors.

To this day we identify the Kentucky fighting man with the preindustrial era: Daniel Boone, the lonely long hunter; Kenton, the intrepid forest scout; George Rogers Clark, the dynamic border captain; Benjamin Logan, the county sheriff and militia colonel; and Isaac Shelby, Richard M. Johnson, and John Adair, militia heroes of the War of 1812 who became prominent political leaders. During the nineteenth century the gentleman duelist and feuding mountaineer clansman sustained the frontier tradition. The Kentucky fighting man of the long rifle era was distinguished by his individualism. He cleared a patch, plowed ground, chopped logs, and hunted game to shelter and feed himself and his family. On occasion he joined with his neighbors, under the loosest of militia organizations, to make fast-moving thrusts against Indians and British. The famous 1813 campaign which culminated in the Battle of the Thames lasted only ninety-four days. On these forays the citizen-soldier of Kentucky was usually led by a captain he and his comrades had commissioned by ballot. Even such leaders as Clark in the 1780s or Shelby in 1813 commanded more by personal example and entreaty than by high rank. Although the frontier Kentuckian's Indian opponents were brave, tough, and skillful, their numbers were few, and their weapons and social organizations were comparatively primitive. So the informal war-making methods of pioneer Kentucky sufficed for the planting of white civilization in the Ohio and Mississippi valleys.

Warfare became a vastly different proposition for the Kentucky fighting man of the industrial age—the subject of this book. After

1815 Kentucky's bloody Indian wars became a distant but cherished memory. By 1861 an emerging spirit of nationalism in Europe and America, together with the growth of a modern political apparatus called "the state," had amplified enormously the economic and social resources upon which governments at war could draw. The machine age had begun its transformation of military logistics, communications, and destructive power. As the first large-scale struggle of the industrial period, the Civil War has been called the first modern war. But the end of the era when major conflicts could be fought to the finish was to come within a century after Appomattox. With the advent in 1945 of nuclear weapons, it appeared that the United States could never again rationally hope to overwhelm its enemies with armed force.

Numerous Kentuckians fought in all of the American wars of the brief age of mass "usable combats." That the Kentucky fighting man of the industrial era seemed less distinctive or picturesque than his pioneer predecessor was understandable, given the impersonal nature of modern warfare. Teamwork is the essence of successful fighting by an industrial society. Armies and fleets live, eat, sleep, march or sail, and fight as teams. Still, they are composed of individuals, who think, feel, and often have to act individually. To perceive them as impersonal blocks to be moved around checkerboards is to distort the reality of war.

The following story is a collective portrayal of Kentucky fighting men from 1861 down to 1945. It focuses on individual soldiers, sailors, and airmen—and on the settings in which they fought. It seeks to show the impact of military service on men in camp, at sea, on the march, in the air, in battle—and in prisoner-of-war compounds. It also addresses the questions of how and why they came to bear arms, and how they preserved a sense of humor, dignity, and individual worth despite serving as anonymous, easily replaced components of immense organizations devoted to killing and destruction.

I have broadened the term "fighting men" to encompass the supporting "tail" of an army or fleet as well as its front-line "head." The experiences of various individuals over most of a century inevitably reflect the unceasing evolution of the art and science of war, the nature of combat, the organization and composition of armed forces, and the attitudes of society at large. To ignore the context in which Kentuckians have fought is to reduce their story to a collection of yarns.

I have emphasized both the citizen-soldier—serving only for the duration of a conflict—and the military careerist, the so-called professional manager of violence. Certain Kentuckians have approached the pinnacle of the calling of arms, and their unending concern with the fundamental military problems of readiness, strategy, leadership, and morale makes them a major part of the story of the Kentuckian as fighting man from the Civil War to World War II.

1

PROUD TO BE ALIVE AND A KENTUCKIAN

For generations "the war" meant to Kentuckians, as to all Americans, the horrendous tragedy unleashed in April 1861 when Maj. Robert Anderson of Louisville hauled down the stars-and-stripes at Fort Sumter. For months the steadfast major and his garrison had sat atop a figurative powder keg that might be exploded at any moment by South Carolina's secessionist fire-eaters. Long denied provisions and reinforcements by the Rebel batteries ringing Charleston harbor, Anderson and his men endured for twenty-four hours the bombardment that began in the early hours of April 12. Their stand placed upon the infant Confederate States of America the moral burden of having fired the first shots of the Civil War. Before Anderson himself once again raised Old Glory over the masonry fort at the harbor's mouth exactly four years after he had surrendered it, the war was to claim the lives of more than 600,000 of its participants. Among its 10,000-plus battles and skirmishes, large and small, some 453 would be fought in Anderson's native Kentucky, more clashes than in five of the Confederate states. Kentucky's 1860 population of 1.15 million, of which 20.4 percent was black, provided perhaps as many as 90,000 Union soldiers. A minimum of 25,000 more bore arms for the South. Small wonder that the fratricidal conflict seared itself into the collective memory of every family and locality of the commonwealth.

What sort of people were these Kentuckians of the borderland between the South and the Old Northwest? What impelled them to flock to the colors? Historically, the citizens of the Bluegrass State had cherished a remarkably contradictory set of values. In the mid-nineteenth century many supported slavery, and most accepted the premise that the Negro was an inferior being. Yet most Kentuckians were at the same time staunchly nationalist patriots who disdained the emerging southern separatism of the 1850s. They had long boasted of the valor of their pioneer forebears, and had regularly bestowed political honors upon the military heroes of the 1812 and Mexican wars. A bewildering mixture of circumstances led Kentuckians into the blue and gray ranks: political and social principles; peer-group pressure; the wish to share the comradeship of camp and battlefield; stern compulsion from the Union army draft; a gritty determination to defend hearth and home; sheer chance—or the desire not to miss the most awesome and terrible event in the history of the nation.

From the summer of 1861 male Kentuckians gravitated into active service. Not all of the new soldiers went gladly. Leitchfield's T. Robert McBeath considered that joining the 27th Kentucky was a duty he would have chosen to avoid had not been convinced that the Union cause was "one to which every patriot should contribute all his energies, and even his life if his country should demand it." Benjamin F. Buckner, a Union officer from Winchester with a Rebel-sympathizing fiancée, hoped that the war would be short, thus resolving his personal predicament. A Confederate invasion of Kentucky led by Braxton Bragg in the autumn of 1862 put Samuel M. Starling, a fifty-five-year-old slaveholding gentleman of leisure from Christian County, into a Federal uniform. Trapped by Bragg's advance in Louisville, where he had gone on business, Starling lounged about the Galt House for a day for two: "I did not know what to do, so I joined, got a Lieut[enant's] Commission and was made . . . Inspector Genl. of Ordnance & Infantry for . . . [Brig. Gen. James S. Jackson's] Division."

A fair number of Kentuckians went involuntarily to war or actively sought to avoid service altogether. The Meade County family of Richard Herndon retained its slaves throughout the war, and in November 1863 went to the polls determined to vote for the "Copperhead" (antiwar Democratic) ticket "if there are not too many Radical bayonets present." In October 1864 Richard satisfied the Federal draft by furnishing a substitute for a year's soldiering. His surrogate was one James Banks, a twenty-two-year-old black whom the law would set free in return for his service.

Unless they lived near the Tennessee line, prospective Kentucky Confederates discovered that it was a major undertaking to proceed through the Union lines. From Indiana, where his Bath County, Kentucky, family had removed in the early 1850s, Henry Lane Stone made his way to Louisville in late 1862. He walked out of the city without a provost marshal's pass, boarded an Ohio steamboat for Augusta, and proceeded south "walking twenty miles in six hours on a rough pike." At a country tavern where Stone sought overnight shelter fourteen Unionist Home Guards "came in and caroused awhile and I had some fears of being captured, but it was not done. This was as far as these puppies then dared to venture" south of the Ohio. Stone joined the 9th (Confederate) Kentucky cavalry on 7 October 1862. "I do not regret the course I have taken and never expect to," he wrote in December. "I believe now as always before we cannot be conquered, nor united with the Yankees again. The Southern people are a unit and Kentucky in the bargain, if left free." Undoubtedly Henry's parents read his letters with mixed emotions; they had three other sons in the Federal army.

The very immensity of the Civil War differentiated it from all earlier American conflicts. As recently as 1846–47 Kentucky's Mexican War share of volunteers had been set at a mere five regiments. The total 1861–65 quota was 100,194 men, and the state was finally credited by the War Department with having furnished 75,275. A technological revolution in the transporting of people, equipment, and commodities indulged the Civil War in its ravenous appetite for manpower. Whereas in the past food, ammunition, and reinforcements were moved forward only by horse- or mule-drawn wagons or primitive river barges, the railroad and steamboat now made it practical for armies of fifty thousand or more men to encamp or campaign in regions once closed to forces of fewer than ten thousand.

Even so, a Civil War army in motion was a ponderous beast.

After the Battle of Perryville, Samuel Starling rode with Maj. Gen. Don Carlos Buell's Army of the Ohio on its listless stern chase of Bragg's Confederates toward Crab Orchard. A march was not simply "like every fellow mounting his horse and riding all day without interruptions," Starling observed. To all brigades would go written orders from the commanding general to take the road the following morning at half-hour intervals. If the first brigade set out at daybreak, the last was unlikely to move before nine o'clock. Following each brigade were ambulances, provisions, and baggage wagons. Fully extended in a marching column, an army of thirty thousand men would be ten miles long. Patrolling the extreme rear were five or six hundred men who had been detached to round up stragglers. "Now comes the tug," Starling pointed out. From each regiment at least fifty men sought constantly to drop out of the ranks at "every turnip patch, persimmon tree, walnut tree or orchard." Despite all efforts to prevent straggling, such men would return to camp the next day "after a night of the most outrageous marauding. They come in loaded with chickens, Geese, honey, and indeed everything they can steal. 'Where did you get them chickens, you damned rascal?' 'Indeed cap, I got them for 25 cents apiece.' . . . No outrage when known at the time of its commission would be tolerated, but the officers are slack in discipline, don't care to trouble themselves about such matters and let them pass with scarce an enquiry."

The purpose of many marches was unfathomable to the men in the ranks and their junior officers. Maj. B. F. Buckner complained on 15 February 1862 that only the day before, his unit, the 20th Kentucky, had moved with "all haste" some nineteen weary miles down the road, only to be hailed by a courier with countermanding orders. Now "we have received orders from Genl Buell . . . to march . . . at once to Louisville—So we start in the morning early. Where we go from there, the Lord knows. We have been marched and countermarched until I am tired of it."

Resting in camp was much deadlier than road marching. Less than 39 percent of all Civil War military-service deaths resulted from battle. By contrast, almost 72 percent of American military fatalities in World War II were combat related. Sheer ignorance caused the 1861–65 deaths: ignorance of dietary requirements, proper medical procedures, and sanitary precautions. Indeed, an army on the move was much more apt to be healthy than a stationary one, and a veteran command, in which only the hardiest physical specimens remained, was less likely to be decimated by illness than an outfit of raw recruits.

Camp-related sickness was a recurrent theme in the writings of Civil War soldiers. In January 1862 Ben Buckner witnessed the death throes of a comrade. The "poor fellow was gasping for breath with the cold sweat of death upon his brow and the death rattle in his throat. . . . Alone, friendless, and unfurnished with the Comforts necessary for the occasion, it is a terrible thing to die. We have lost several men whose deaths were . . . the result of inattention and incompetence . . . of the attending physician. This is the worst thing in the army and makes me sick at heart."

Conditions were even more bleak for the 14th Kentucky in the remote valley of the Big Sandy. From Paintsville, Arch Means of Ashland lamented that this "is a miserable place for a Camp,—and if this wet weather continues a great proportion [of our men] will be unfit for duty.—We are doing nothing but lay around camp." Only when the camp was moved to "a sloping, and *sodded* piece of ground," did sickness in the regiment begin to decline. Means was hopeful that he had left Paintsville behind for good: "We are still in sight of that place, if you choose to look in that direction." But at least his regiment was out of the mud for the time being.

Experience in the field made soldiers increasingly adept in sheltering themselves. From Russellville, Union cavalryman Thomas Speed reported in February 1863 that he and two comrades had made their hut remarkably comfortable. With spare tentflies they had improvised a makeshift front porch to keep the wind away from the door. Inside, a small stove was equal to any chill. Speed slept on a cob bed, while his compatriots stretched out on straw. "The truth is," Speed declared, "I find it harder to be comfortable when awake than when asleep—Camp is certainly a monotonous place. . . . Selfishness reigns supreme, and one man is treated just like another except when all the parties are *well* known to each other. . . . In camp idleness is the prevailing employment. And *food* for conversations becomes scarce. Public matters have become a hackneyed topic. The weather won't near do. So you will see men who were old acquaintances gather together in societies, and strangers cannot mix with pleasure."

Kentucky's Civil War soldiers found in the sutler's wagon at least a primitive version of the twentieth-century Post Exchange. The sutler purveyed "a plentiful supply of wine and beer," which thousands of soldiers undeniably regarded as an effective means of banishing homesickness, boredom, fatigue, and fear. During his long months as a staff officer in Bowling Green, Samuel Starling received several demijohns of bourbon whiskey from friends and supplicants among the local citizenry. He forwarded, "*uninspected*," a couple to his daughters, but doubtless kept and enjoyed others.

No mere convivial occasion was a carousal in Giles County, Tennessee, witnessed by Robert McBeath. Asleep in his tent on a July day in 1862, McBeath woke to the sound of "some loud talking . . . and . . . found quite a number of Officers had gathered together before the Colonel's tent over a bucket of ale, which, having passed several times, was being felt seriously by several." McBeath was disgusted with their "loud, boistrous talking, each one talking at the most rapid rate, and nobody listening to anything that was said. . . . After dinner I found that almost half the camp was on a spree, several Officers and many privates being dead drunk."

Religious services, especially those of the "old time" variety, were a more constructive emotional solace for soldiers than liquor. "Sabbath duties" were the principal interest of Presbyterian ministerial aspirant Lt. Thomas Gunn of Lexington. From the 21st Kentucky, Gunn sent home for his provisional preaching license and a *"Book of Psalms in Phonography."* "Oh! how do the soldiers appreciate preaching? You would scarcely believe your own eyes," he remarked in December 1862. And Robert McBeath, aware that Rebel guerrillas and the raiders of John Hunt Morgan were currently plaguing his homeland, mused that "surely Kentucky must have been sinful in other days . . . to suffer [so] much from . . . the present war."

If nourishment of the spirit was beneficial, nourishment of the body was essential to a good morale among Kentucky's Civil War soldiers, as among the soldiers of all wars. Mostly rural in origin, the Kentuckians were accustomed to the plain, hearty eating fare of the family farm. For the Union forces rations were plentiful so long as the supply lines flowed freely. Unfortunately, however, incompetent company cooks often prepared meals that were virtually inedible. Finding food was often a problem during active operations. On the march toward Corinth, Mississippi, in May and June of 1862 with Maj. Gen. Henry W. Halleck's Union force, Robert McBeath complained that "no one who is at home enjoying the peace and quiet and luxuries of life can form any idea of the privations endured by our soldiers in the field. . . . The men frequently march ahead of the wagons, doing without their tents for a week or more at a time [and] having their provisions along in their haversacks. This thing of living on fat meat and bread alone for weeks and weeks without any other change of food is too bad to think about, and much worse to realize."

The army's rough food could be especially hard upon the sick, as Arch Means discovered in January 1862. "I am better today," he wrote, "but have been eating nothing but hard crackers and drinking tea for two days." Means's whole company had suffered from diarrhea. Later that spring a Union advance to Cumberland Gap placed Arch's regiment at the end of a hopelessly long supply line: "Provisions are very scarce, not a day passing without our being entirely out of [one] or more of the necessaries of life.—We are mostly out of hard bread, and this country affords none."

For Confederate soldiers, finding rations was much more of a hit-or-miss proposition than for Unionists. The primitive southern railway system and the eventual worthlessness of Confederate currency made it hard to provision even an encamped army. Thus it was often essential for Rebels to live off the country while in the field. This could be hazardous. One day after the Battle of Perryville Lt. Milton B. Cox reported from Lexington that "we had one Deth this morning from being poisoned as is thought. He eat his breckfast in the country and came to camp and was Dead in less than one hour with out any one knowing it." Foraging is a constant theme in the diary of J. D. Sprake of the 8th (Confederate) Kentucky Cavalry, a semipartisan outfit which moved in a desultory fashion around the eastern foothills. On 29 April 1863 Sprake went foraging for food at the house of a Union man, who "was not *at home.*" From the man's wife he "took meat and meal a'plenty [and] after receiving . . . a quantity of abuse, we departed for the camp. . . . We had a perfect feast, a large kettle of Burgou." In the southeastern part of the state Henry Lane Stone and the Rebel troopers of the 9th Kentucky found that it was possible to ride "ten & fifteen miles without seeing a house and when you did see one it was a little eight by ten log-cabin, with an old woman & nine or ten tow-headed children. . . . Ask them for something to eat and the eatables would be 'plenty but jist out.' "

Kentucky's Civil War soldiers were never sorrier for themselves than when contemplating their lack of feminine companionship. Frequently, they badgered wives and sweethearts who failed to write. Proclaimed one, "An affectionate letter from you is like the Sunbeams to a man who has long been imprisoned in a dark, damp, dismal dungeon, where not a ray of light penetrated, to cheer his sad and oppressed heart." From prosouthern Russellville, Benjamin H. Bristow of the 8th Kentucky Cavalry lamented in March 1863 that "a Federal officer can only tell by the occasional glimpse of a slim pattern of 'calico' as it darts like a meteor . . . that female humanity dwells in 'these parts.' It has been my fortune once or twice . . . to meet on the public street a walking, moving form in female attire. . . . Such ghostly looks, such wolfish ferocity of countenance & expressions of fiendish animosity are too much for my weak nerves." Other officers in Bristow's regiment managed to bridge the bitterness of war and make social contacts in Russellville. Their perseverance was understandable, for as B. F. Buckner observed in nearby Bowling Green, "Any sort of ladies' society is sought by soldiers with an avidity that can only be understood by one who has been a soldier. Even the most dull and uninteresting specimens of the sex become belles in the neighborhood of our Camps." It should be noted that there are remarkably few documented cases of physical violence suffered by women at the hands of Civil War soldiers.

Whichever side they had originally embraced, the Kentuckians of 1861–65 found their respective loyalties sorely challenged by the growing viciousness of the struggle. The Confederacy's hopeless plight was increasingly evident to its fighting men. One such person was a seventeen-year-old described in November 1862 by Samuel Starling at Bowling Green. His one-year enlistment had obviously given the lad a surfeit of soldiering, and he wanted nothing more than to return home. The Union district commander would at first have none of it: "By God sir, you ought to be hung. I can't permit such fellows to come sneaking back and live undisturbed in our lines. I'll have you arrested, and imprisoned, sir." But the next morning Starling quietly gained the general's permission to handle the case: "It was the first look, or word, of sympathy . . . [that the boy] had had from the crowd of shoulder-strapped gentry . . . and he burst into a hearty fit of crying." Starling later released the youth into the custody of his sisters upon their posting a five-hundred-dollar bond.

Kentucky's Unionists found themselves in an awkward position on the winning side. Unlike many compatriots from beyond the Ohio, they did not necessarily hate the South or southerners. Robert McBeath found Iuka, Mississippi, to be a "beautiful place." He took at their word such southerners as a Middle Tennessee woman "whose husband lived with her only eight days after their marriage" before going into the Confederate army: "She said she did not care how the affair ended, if she could only get her husband back safe." In November 1864 Col. Hubbard Milward of the 18th (Union) Kentucky wrote that "Atlanta burning presents a splendid spectacle. . . . This town burning is, I suppose, necessary, but [I] regret its being done."

All normal civil-military tensions increased several-fold when the armies operated inside Kentucky. For a time early in 1862 Maj. B. F. Buckner's Union regiment was stationed at Smithland, near where many of its men had been recruited. "Each officer and a large proportion of the men," Buckner complained, "are continually soliciting me to permit some expedition to . . . avenge some insult or wrong that their friends have suffered at the hands of the Secesh." Buckner himself became angry with a Rebel sympathizer several weeks later in Simpson County. Buckner requested a drink of water at a farmhouse. Gruffly replying that he had none, the owner hustled three slaves into the house, locking the door behind them. "I was of course in a very bad humor," Buckner related, "and was on the point of making some angry reply when I looked around & saw about 50 of the 2nd Ky. going into his cabbage and, knowing what would be the fate of the cabbage, I felt that my revenge was complete."

In the fall of 1862 Samuel Starling denounced "the cursed Yankees who compose our army. They appear to believe that there are no Loyal men in our State." Four months later Starling's views were unchanged: "I wish the cursed Yankees were out of the Country! No good feeling has grown out of their occupancy of our State, but a dissimilarity the most striking is manifest in the way they feel and think about everything."

President Lincoln's Emancipation Proclamation, published in September 1862, was the sternest nonbattle dilemma to confront Kentucky's blue-clad soldiers, most of whom fought to preserve the nation—not to abolish the "peculiar institution of the South." The proclamation did not immediately affect the slaves of Kentucky, being directed instead at those areas still in rebellion as of 1 January 1863, but its long-term implications were not to be doubted. Benjamin Buckner's reaction to the proclamation was entirely in character. It was "a most abominable, infamous document" that falsified all of Lincoln's previous pronouncements on slavery: "The Union Kentuckians are most shamefully treated, and by . . . the president's want of good faith, which is only equalled by his lack of sense, we find ourselves in arms to maintain doctrines, which, if announced 12 months ago, would have driven us all, notwithstanding our loyalty to the Constitution & the Union, into the ranks of the Southern Army." Ben Buckner had reached a critical personal decision about the war; he would abandon it: "I have no hope that my resignation will be accepted, but I intend to tender it whenever we . . . [receive] orders to leave the state."

Still, no matter how much the Union soldiers of Kentucky loathed the crusade against slavery, they gradually came to hate even more those Kentuckians who collaborated with Confederate soldiers or guerrillas. In March 1863, weary of "individuals who stroll about the country stirring up Sedition, stealing private property, burning bridges," Benjamin Bristow issued orders to his cavalry troopers "to take no more prisoners unless they surrender . . . in [the] open. Our motto now is, if a fellow isn't worth shooting, he isn't worth taking prisoner." Gradually, Samuel Starling embraced the hard-war animosities of his friend Bristow. Out of uniform in October 1863, he was galled to "see so many damned rascals walking about town [in Hopkinsville]. . . . There ought to be a standing gallows & a Rebel hung every county court day; such an exhibition would have a fine effect on the spectators, and would be a vast saving in blood and treasure."

The momentum of the war swept along those Kentucky Unionists who stayed with the colors. Many officers of the 21st Kentucky, Thomas Gunn noted in December 1862, had "been complaining and murmuring . . . on account of alleged interferences in Ky. with private property (niggers). . . . I believe . . . that they are just tired of the Service & are trying to find a pretext for resigning so as to go home & live off their kin & spend what little they have made off of U[ncle] S[am]." By March 1863 Gunn had come to "believe God will never let our nation rest until Slavery is annihilated." It was time for the Bluegrass State to come to terms with the death of slavery and get on with the war. Such were the sentiments of Col. E. H. Murray, in command of a cavalry brigade with the army of Maj. Gen. William T. Sherman. In May 1864 Murray professed himself a proud man, "in the first place because I am alive; in the next place that I am a Kentuckian. . . . Kentucky's Loyalty can never be doubted. Her record is a proud one, and one which will ever give honor to us all."

Often more plainly than their senior commanders, Kentucky's junior officers and common soldiers of 1861–65 perceived that armies exist for combat and that wars are won by fighting. While they dreaded the violence, din, shock, stark terror, mortal dangers, and physical and emotional exhaustion of the battlefield, they were surprisingly willing to undergo the ordeal of combat—provided always that their sacrifices were intelligently directed toward worthwhile and winnable objectives. Battered hard in the 1862–63 midwinter Battle of Stone's River in Middle Tennessee, "our men . . . [nevertheless] have a desire once again to try Rosecrans's Army," said C. W. Fackler, who came of Kentucky stock and belonged to an Alabama regiment of Confederates. Months passed before the hoped-for battle was finally fought—at Chickamauga in northwestern Georgia. So stupendous was that two-day collision of 125,000 armed men that it was hard for participants to envision exactly what had taken place. Not surprisingly, A. W. Randolph, a member of the famous Orphan Brigade of Kentucky Confederates, could not find the words for more than a laconic description of the battle: "Last Sunday we meet the enemy at Chickamawga River and routed them. Drove them back to Chattanooga. . . . Our Brigade took during the day 9 pieces of Artilary. . . . The Charge of our Division is the greatest thing of the war. . . . It was us that started them. Gen. Breckinridge was up with and through the line during the Charge. Gen. Ben Hardin Helm of Louisville and Lt. Col. Hewitt were killed. . . . Our loss pretty heavy. . . . Our men all went into the fight with a great determination to conquer. The Lord has given us a great victory in this fight and we cannot be to[o] thankful to him for it. . . . In our company we had one man killed and Five wounded."

As one man among many thousands in the ranks, Randolph could hardly have been expected to comprehend from his personal vantage point the overall progress of the great Battle of Chickamauga. But along with the rest of Maj. Gen. John C. Breckinridge's division the Orphan Brigade had in fact made a vital contribution to the Confederate triumph by delivering on the morning of 20 September 1863 a fierce assault against the flank and rear of Maj. Gen. George H. Thomas's left wing of the Federal army. So hard-pressed were Thomas's men that Maj. Gen. William S. Rosecrans, the Union commander, felt compelled to shift troops from the right to reinforce Old Pap's XIV Corps. Later that day the weakened Federal right was shattered and driven from the field by a powerful stroke from Lt. Gen. James Longstreet's Rebel corps. Thus the action in which Randolph had participated amounted to an important holding attack—if not quite the "greatest thing of the war" as he had claimed.

In the Civil War any successful charge was noteworthy. Most infantry attacks failed, and against entrenched defenders there was almost no chance of success. By 1863 the soldiers of both sides instinctively fortified any point at which they were halted for more than an hour or so whether they had orders to entrench or not.

Moreover, recent improvements in small arms had precipitated a revolution in battlefield tactics as far-reaching as the concurrent logistical revolution. Most Civil War infantrymen carried muzzle-loading muskets with rifled barrels. Their rate of fire was two to six rounds per minute, but their killing range was up to five hundred yards—several times the range of the smoothbore muskets upon which the bayonet-oriented infantry tactics of the mid-nineteenth century were based. Fired as they were by percussion caps, the new weapons functioned much more reliably than had their flintlock predecessors, even in wet weather. Besides mowing down exposed infantrymen who stormed well-defended positions, the new rifles also rendered obsolete the winning of battles through climactic charges by massed cavalry. On the other hand, artillery organization and fire-control techniques were still comparatively primitive, and the guns themselves still relatively short-ranged and inaccurate, so Civil War cannon were much more effective at disrupting enemy assaults than at softening up defensive positions. The officers of 1861–65 sensed—if not always clearly—the nature of the tactical problems posed by the new dominance of the battlefield by entrenched riflemen, and throughout the conflict they groped uncertainly for solutions.

From the outset of the war the troops recognized that there were two kinds of soldiers: those who had been in battle and those who had not. The initiated were sometimes described as men who had "seen the elephant," a wondrously exotic beast in nineteenth-century eyes. No Civil War soldier doubted that his first exposure to combat was a major event of his life. Arch Means first heard enemy fire at Middle Creek early in 1862, although he could hardly be called a participant in the action. Nevertheless, he was sufficiently moved to compose an exhaustive account of the clash. Arch's 14th Kentucky received orders on the evening of January 9 to move at daybreak as part of a fourteen-hundred-man reinforcement of Col. James A. Garfield's advance force of eleven hundred. A *"hard march"* brought the men to Abbott Hill, near Prestonsburg, early in the following afternoon. Resting, Arch and his compatriots suddenly heard resounding through the hills the rumble of a cannon some three or four miles in the distance. The entire command hastened toward the sound "as fast as our wearied feet could carry us, but that was slow." Ahead of Arch's regiment, the 40th Ohio was sending up "cheer after cheer that made the hills ring." On the ridge in the distance Means could see a large body of men, and he realized that they were the enemy. The Rebels fell back toward "the highest point of the Ridge," where it appeared that the "hardest and hottest part of the battle" was taking place. The Union artillery "kept up a constant firing, at what I could not exactly tell, except that occasionally a shot . . . would be heard in the air near to us, and above our heads." The clash lasted more than three hours. That night a "contraband" reported that the Rebels had withdrawn. A reconnaissance the next morning confirmed the Negro's story. His feet being sore from the previous day's march, Arch did not visit the battlefield. Others who did claimed to have discovered "unmistakable signs of great slaughter," although no bodies were in evidence.

As exciting as it had been to Arch Means and his fellow soldiers, Middle Creek amounted in truth to little more than a skirmish. Only a few men on both sides had fallen, although for a time the action was brisk as about eight hundred of Garfield's men sought to drive those of Humphrey Marshall off their hilly perch. Inaccurate firearms, atrocious marksmanship, and rugged hillside terrain largely explain the paucity of bloodshed. Even so, the engagement's noise, spectacle, and the conflicting—but overpowering—sensations of elation, fear, exhaustion, and hunger transcended any of the experiences of Arch's youth. The aftermath of battle was anticlimactic for all of the participants. Both sides withdrew from the field, each claiming a victory. Neither could have sustained a campaign, given the impossibility of supplying forces of any size in the inhospitable Big Sandy country.

Over the next few months Means sorted out in his mind the details of his brief exposure to combat at Middle Creek. When next he saw action, near Cumberland Gap at the beginning of May 1862, his account of the fighting was much more restrained. Ordered with his company to hurry toward the sound of musket and cannon fire, Arch found the Union combatants deployed behind logs, stumps, rocks, and trees along the top of a ridge that faced

Confederate fortifications some three hundred yards away. Rebel bullets whistled overhead, but the men who fired them were well concealed: "Upon looking a little longer, I could see a head pop up, and then another, above the embankment thrown up around the top of the mountain—Our boys would crawl up to the top of the ridge, lay flat on the ground and the most cool would wait until they could get sight, and then fire, but some of them might as well have fired into the air." Despite the extreme range and difficulty of spotting targets, the Federal troops directed a volume of fire sufficient to silence what appears to have been a single Rebel cannon. The skirmish was insignificant, and the Unionists were soon ordered to retire.

Civil War soldiers hazarded their lives in dozens of firefights for each time they fought in a full-scale battle. Indeed, participants frequently described General Sherman's four-month Atlanta campaign of 1864 as "a big Indian war." Although the long advance included only about four major battles, not a day passed without continuous maneuvering and large-scale skirmishing. Capt. Thomas Speed long afterward recalled leading a company of skirmishers ahead of a larger formation. Moving out from the cover of a grove of trees, "we discovered that our forces were advancing in line of battle from the woods we had just left. A simultaneous shout went up from the advancing columns and the skirmishers, and we pressed forward to the enemy's line. They gave us the loads they had in their guns and then abandoned their work and fled the woods. Our skirmishers captured a few prisoners and occupied the position held by the enemy. We claimed to have won it and no one disputed our claim. . . . I mention this affair . . . because during the summer of 1864 we had many of like character, of which there never will . . . be any history."

Very often the hazards of Civil War combat were as deadly for generals and staff aides as for the men in the ranks. James Jackson, Samuel Starling's general at the Battle of Perryville, was slain, and Starling himself was "sickened with this cursed strife. . . . I cannot attempt a description of the battlefield, the poor dust-covered, ghastley looking fellows dead in every posture, some with heads half shot off, and some with their knapsacks under their heads and over their faces, evidently adjusted by themselves before death. Altogether, there is a horrible, sickening feeling produced beyond anything I ever before felt."

Not for a month could Starling bring himself to compose an "egotistical, confidential" narrative of his experiences at Perryville. Jackson's division had hurried toward the sound of cannon fire. The general posted his troops near a house, and dismounted in the yard with his subordinate commanders and staff. Starling noted that "the bottle was pretty freely circulated among the officers." As the artillery fire intensified, the officers dispersed to their respective commands, but the "flash and smoke" of the guns suggested that the enemy was still at least a mile away. "Creeping through the weeds, their dress so of the color of grass that you could hardly see them," the Confederates reached a rail fence only 150 yards from one of Jackson's brigades before being detected. The "peculiar whizzing noise" overhead of "Minnie balls" prompted Jackson to remark, "Well, I'll be damned if this is not getting rather particular." Those were his last words, for in a moment he was struck dead only three yards from the horrified Starling. The general's black servant was also killed. Jackson's eyes "were closed with a tightness [that was] preternatural. His eyebrows almost rested on his cheeks—his mouth was open, and he gave several short spasmodic groans, but I am sure he breathed *not once.*" Starling and another officer carried the heavy body of their fallen commander to the bottom of a hill, and went off to find an ambulance. While they were gone the Confederates temporarily overran the spot where the body lay, but it was back in Federal hands by the next morning. Starling returned to the body: "We found quite a number of Rebel & Union soldiers, ministering to the wounded and looking at the [battle]ground. All animosity had ceased & they were mixing like friends. We found Jackson just where we left him, laid out very straight, with his boots, hat & buttons taken, but his body untouched. We put him in an ambulance & dashed on towards Louisville."

The slain Jackson was one of no fewer than seventy-nine Kentucky-born generals of the Civil War: forty-one Union and thirty-eight Confederate. In all, six Kentucky generals were killed in battle and five more died of other causes before the end of the conflict.

Although no army can function without intelligent direction, capable leaders were in critically short supply during the Civil War. Over its first six decades the United States Military Academy produced only 1,966 graduates. Thus West Pointers were in the minority among the generals of 1861-65. No Civil War officer on either side had received any postgraduate military education such as that already being conducted by the Great General Staff of Prussia. Very few American officers had chosen to undertake on their own any systematic study of their profession. Moreover, during the hectic mobilization of 1861-62 neither side thought to establish officer-candidate schools. Indeed, company commanders were often elected by the volunteers under their command, and many regiments were mustered into service with gubernatorial political appointees at their heads. No Civil War field commander had handled anything larger than a regiment before 1861, and the armies of 1861-65 were usually five to ten times as large as any American army of the past. So it is not surprising that Civil War units were led by grizzled, sometimes narrow-minded career soldiers from the skeleton Old Army of the Indian wars, or by ambitious, glory-hunting politicians, or by patriotic hometown leading citizens lacking any military experience. The surprise is that these ill-prepared leaders performed as well as they did, and that they so quickly transformed the "improvised war" of 1861-62 into the "organized war" of 1863-65.

Many newly minted Civil War officers were painfully aware of their poor qualifications. For instance the Kentuckian Jeremiah T. Boyle, who for some unfathomable reason had been made a Union brigadier, protested to General Buell, "I have *no* knowledge of military tactics—I never gave even the order to Shoulder arms—I never attempted to drill a soldier—I never saw a company or battalion drilled one half hour. . . . I have no ambition to gratify at the expense of the cause . . . or the lives of its soldiers. I shall willingly give place to any competent man of experience." Another ill-prepared officer was Col. Laban T. Moore of Arch Mean's 14th Kentucky. Early in 1862 Arch complained that the regiment "is nearly demoralized, & if we are not sent into some Camp of Instruction, I have but little hopes of our doing any good hereafter.—Our staff officers are sadly deficient. . . . Our quartermaster does as he pleases, and thinks nobody is his superior—We want a man, a head to this regiment." Fortunately for Moore's men, Arch was soon able to report that the colonel had acknowledged the bad situation by voluntarily making way for a more capable successor: "Of course our Lieut. Col. or Major could not see any cause for their resigning."

Soldiers soon realized that commanders who displayed concern for the welfare of their troops were also the most likely to succeed in combat. Arch Means's brigade commander, the Ohio politician and future President James A. Garfield, was "a good man," Arch thought. Garfield "is energetic and endeavors to take care of his men."

Physical cowardice was the one failing Civil War soldiers refused to tolerate in their superiors. "*Threatened* with sickness" at the Battle of Shiloh in West Tennessee in April 1862, Col. Sanders Bruce of Ben Buckner's 20th Kentucky left his unit "about 11 o'clock on the morning of the fight, & did not return until that night after the fight was over & we were in camp, and then only stayed a few minutes, but went to the landing and went on board a steamboat & went to Savannah [Tennessee] & did not return until next day about noon."

A very human and more forgivable shortcoming than cowardice was posturing by high-ranking officers. The keen-eyed, acid-penned Samuel Starling considered Lovell H. Rousseau, a Kentucky general and a "large fiery nosed man," to be a "demagogue and a sensationalist." At Perryville, "draped in all the finery of war, ostrich feathers, gold lace, &c," Rousseau "dashed down the line in a rapid gallop, with a stern theatrical smile on his face and looked more like the flying Indian in the circus than anything." Rousseau held his hat on a pointed sword. His ride was hardly heroic because his troops were not under fire when it took place. Starling thought "it quite probable that the great general (yet to be) of this war, is now a noncommissioned officer, or possibly a private."

Kentucky's total of native-born generals ranked behind only

Virginia and New York, but no Bluegrass soldier won a place among the "great" Civil War commanders. Kentucky did furnish two of the Confederacy's eight full generals: Albert Sidney Johnston of Washington and John Bell Hood of Owingsville, both of whom were adoptive Texans at the outbreak of the war. Johnston's date of rank preceded even that of R. E. Lee, and President Jefferson Davis rated him as the South's most promising soldier. Given the impossible task in the fall of 1861 of holding with minimum strength a long and vulnerable line across southern Kentucky, Johnston had to abandon not only that line but also most of Middle and West Tennessee after the fall early in 1862 of forts Henry and Donelson. Nevertheless, Johnston struck back, catching U.S. Grant's Army of the Tennessee completely by surprise at Shiloh on April 6. Going personally to the hottest of the fighting, Johnston was hit and soon bled to death. After another day of battle the Confederates retreated. The South bewailed its loss of an undeniably gallant soldier, but after the war Johnston's reputation shriveled under the criticism of historians. Actualy, he died too early in the war for a fair appraisal of his merits. With experience he might have displayed strategic gifts and become proficient at handling a large army.

If Johnston's tenure in command was too brief for evaluation, John Bell Hood's was not. As a brigade and division chieftain in Lee's Army of Northern Virginia during 1862–63, Hood was probably the Confederacy's stoutest battlefield paladin. Lee habitually counted on Hood and his men to strike home in the toughest fighting. By 1864 the battle-maimed Hood had risen above his talents to become a corps commander in the Army of Tennessee. Taking command of the army in July, Hood vainly tried to save Atlanta from Sherman's grasp by a series of hopeless and ineptly managed headlong assaults. After the fall of Atlanta he led a desperate offensive into Tennessee against the Union rear. His army was virtually destroyed in November and December of 1864 at the catastrophic battles of Franklin and Nashville. His troops ruefully sang that "the gallant Hood of Texas played hell in Tennessee." In short, Hood's magnificent physique and bravery made him an ideal subordinate comander, a level at which he should have been kept because of his intellectual limitations.

A Louisville native who had long since moved to Illinois, John Pope was the only Kentucky-born commander of a full-size Union field army. Pope's braggadocio and caustic tongue gained him innumerable enemies, especially among conservative Democratic friends of Maj. Gen. George B. McClellan, who commanded the Army of the Potomac early in the war. Those critics, and Pope's harsh reprisals against civilian harassers of the Federal rear, won him the support of the congressional Republican antislavery Radicals. Following modest successes in the Mississippi Valley, notably including the capture early in 1862 of Island No. 10, Pope was shifted to the East. There, in the second Battle of Bull Run at the end of August 1862, he was completely outgeneraled by R. E. Lee. Pope bitterly blamed his defeat uppon McClellan's friends among the eastern generals, but he was not again entrusted with command against the Confederates. His valuable Republican connections nevertheless won for him permanent postwar rank as a brigadier general and long frontier service as a department commander. Although Pope was ahead of his time in comprehending the 1861–65 struggle as a "total" war, his professional ceilling, like that of Hood, was as a brigade or division commander.

A far more vivid figure in the folklore of the Bluegrass State than Johnston, Hood, or Pope was the charismatic Rebel cavalryman John Hunt Morgan. The scion of a prominent Lexington family, Morgan repeatedly galloped through Kentucky on swift raids, the strategic value of which was nonexistent. His boldest stroke, executed in defiance of orders, was a midsummer 1863 "big raid" that covered eleven hundred miles and ended in Ohio with the capture of Morgan and 335 of his men only sixty miles from Lake Erie. With a few companions, the resourceful Morgan escaped from the Ohio state penitentiary and took to the field again, to be slain near Greeneville, Tennessee, in September 1864. Morgan evinced no skills as an administrator or disciplinarian, nor did he have the capacity to work in harness with other commanders and formations. Morgan did possess personal bravery and magnetism, modest talents which, if enhanced by West Point training and regular-army experience, might have made him a useful officer—at least in a subordinate capacity.

In contrast to Morgan, the now-obscure John Buford turned

out to be one of the most effective cavalrymen of the Civil War. A Woodford County-born Unionist who, like Pope, had been appointed to West Point from Illinois, Buford was a veteran of more than a decade of hard service on the frontier. At the crisis of the war Buford led a cavalry division in the Army of the Potomac. At Brandy Station, Virginia, in June 1863, and at Gettysburg a few weeks later, he demonstrated his mastery of "dragoon tactics": moving swiftly on horseback to seize vital terrain, then dismounting to defend it with light artillery and the rapid-fire Spencer carbine until relieved by the infantry. Buford's two-hour holding action west of Gettysburg during the early hours of 1 July 1863 was essential to the Union triumph. Months later the Kentucky-born general died of the cumulative effects of wounds and exhaustion.

The concentration by students of the Civil War upon its battles and leaders has obscured the melancholy fate of the men who were captured. From start to finish there were 674,045 men taken on both sides. As they had shared in the high drama of battle, so, too, did the soldiers of Kentucky participate fully in the low ordeal of the prison camp. One of many Confederates caught during Morgan's raid into Indiana and Ohio, J. D. Sprake of the 8th Kentucky Cavalry recorded that he and his compatriots had ridden into a trap: "Tonight I am a prisoner. No human being can describe my feelings. We are all in a square wheat field heavily guarded, but in spite of the circumstances [I] fell asleep and slept soundly all night." Captured at the same time was Henry Lane Stone, who soon escaped from Camp Douglas, Illinois, by climbing over its fence. Aided by his brother, a Chicago medical student, he got southward and made his way to the former home of his family in Bath County, Kentucky. There, a Dr. Sharp, once a family friend, brought a party of Unionists to recapture Henry: "When they surrounded the house, I was sitting in the 'lower room,' boots blacked, shaved, and a clean shirt, and flattering myself I was safe. . . . I had no arms with me, and so I walked out . . . [and] said, 'How are you, Doctor,' and told him I was his prisoner. But I thought it was hard to be taken right on the spot where I was born; and that too by a former friend of our family, for no other crime than that I had been defending from oppression my native soil, the very home of my fathers." Stone eluded his captors before they could get him to a prison camp, and this time he reached Canada safely. "The women all skate here," he noted upon arrival. "[You] can see their ankles easy." Months later Stone finally rejoined the Confederate army.

Comparatively few Kentuckians succeeded in escaping from captivity. And for most of the last two years of the war the Union government refused to exchange prisoners of war with the manpower-shy South. The Confederate camp at Andersonville, Georgia, was the most notorious incarceration center of the war, but most Federal camps were almost equally grim, and with much less justification. Unlike the Confederates, the northern authorities could have improved prisoner accommodations, medical care, and rations had they wanted to. Mount Sterling's Robert T. Bean, late of the 8th Kentucky Cavalry in Morgan's command, endured seventeen bleak months at Camp Douglas and discovered that the constant struggle to tunnel out, or at least get more food and a few luxuries, became an obsession. Bean and several companions arranged with a woman, who came daily to peddle milk from a tin can with a long spout, to close off the spout with a cork and "fill the can with whiskey [and] the spout with milk," so that the liquor could be smuggled past the guards. Another time, recalled Bean, a Chicago woman rode to Camp Douglas behind a "pair of high stepping Kentucky bays." The "aristocratic lady" was followed closely by her "aristocratic dog." While she was denouncing the Confederate cause, the prisoners inveigled her dog "into the barrack, which he never left. His flesh was pronounced first class, and sharp lookouts were kept for more of his kind."

An angel of mercy at Camp Douglas was Mary Blackburn Morris, a Woodford County native married to a resident of Chicago. Morris brought medicine, food, and bedclothes to prisoners and even helped some of them to escape. She was eventually arrested and banished back to Kentucky by the Federal authorities.

The passing months weighted down prisoners with despair. In September 1864 J. D. Sprake lamented that "rations are very short, great suffering from hunger, many seem almost wild, bread can't be got for love nor money. . . . O, how I long for freedom and once more an equal chance with Yankee blue bellies." Sprake was unwilling either to join the Union army or to give his oath to the national government: "Never will I swear so base a lie, as allegiance to U.S., ruled by such a tyrant as Abe Lincoln. No, I am a southern man and will live and die one, and true to my country." A fair number of Sprake's prison mates were less adamant than he: "I know some of them swore to a lie just to get out of this place."

All tribulations finally pass. From a Confederate stockade in western Louisiana in October 1864, feeling "like a bird just escaped," W. H. Cundiff and fellow prisoners started off toward Baton Rouge for exchange and freedom. Once he reached home in Somerset, Kentucky, no Rebel sympathizers had "better fool with me," Cundiff warned, "for I have taken a slight peep at the elephant myself." But in retrospect "I must say as justice to the guards that guarded us . . . most of them were as kind as they could conveniently bee. I am allways willen to give the devel his due."

The war itself finally ended. The symbolic drama of Lee's capitulation at Appomattox on 9 April 1865 has clouded the fact that Confederate resistance had been gradually diminishing for many months. An estimated 304,000 participants from both sides, including a roughly proportional share of Kentuckians, simply abandoned the struggle by deserting.

Col. Hubbard Milward and his men of the 18th Kentucky found the last months of the struggle totally unlike anything that had gone before. From November 1864 to April 1865 they marched with Sherman's army of sixty thousand on its sweep from Atlanta to Savannah and northward through the Carolinas. Against negligible opposition a blue-clad force ripped a path of devastation through the heart of the South. Milward himself supervised the destruction of the Georgia state arsenal at Milledgeville. Farther down the road he recorded that "language cannot describe the joy of the negroes on the plantations, they thinking themselves free. I warned them the Yankees could do but little for them now."

One of about a dozen Confederate parolees en route to Richmond, Robert Bean reached Salem, in southwestern Virginia, on 10 April 1865, when word came of Lee's surrender the day before. After a "short, but unanimous," council of war the little party started southward where Gen. Joseph E. Johnston was still in the field with the fragments of the old Army of Tennessee. A crippled ankle caused Bean, with one companion, to tarry behind. Within a few days they reached North Carolina, where on the front porch of a farmhouse they noticed "a bottle of peach brandy, golden with age, and by it a loaf of bread with a roll of butter." The owner of the house urged the two travellers to start home: "The war is over; fighting is now a thing of the past, and work will be the rule for many years to come." Recognizing the man's wisdom, Bean and his friend began the long, weary trek back toward Kentucky.

Henry Lane Stone stood by the Lost Cause to the bitter end. Back in the Confederate cavalry in early 1865, he wrote from Johnston's army that "we are now out of S.C. and in the Old North State. Active times [are] in store for the future till Sherman is defeated." By then Johnston's troops had demonstrated their inability to prevent either the fall of Columbia or the invasion of North Carolina. Retreating through Raleigh on April 12, Henry observed that the "people [are still] loyal and dread the approach of the Yanks." But two days later he recorded in Greensboro "rumors upon rumors of the surrender of Gen. Lee & utter demoralization. The rumors are pretty generally believed. Dark, dark indeed seems our cause if all is true we hear." With the small mounted escort of Kentucky troopers that accompanied the fugitive President Davis as far as Washington, Georgia, Henry learned there of "Gen. Johnston's order & terms of surrender; [I] find there is no other mode of conduct but to take a parole."

The return home of some Kentucky Confederates was long delayed. John C. Breckinridge, a former vice-president of the United States who later had been a Confederate major general and secretary of war, accompanied General Joe Johnston on 18 April 1865 to discuss surrender terms with Sherman in Durham County, North Carolina. Then, with President Davis's party, Breckinridge fled southward, and he eventually escaped to Europe by way of Florida and Cuba. Not until President Andrew Johnson issued a sweeping amnesty proclamation at the end of 1868 did Breckinridge conclude that he could return to Lexington. At that he was more fortunate than many Kentucky soldiers of the recent conflict. Perhaps a third of all of those who had borne arms never came back.

Although thousands of men from the Bluegrass State had fought, they made little of a special imprint on the combat history of the Civil War. Kentucky regiments battled all across the western theater, but usually they were brigaded with outfits from other states. General Sherman after the war spoke in very warm terms of the Louisville Legion, a regiment in his army, but the Confederate Orphan Brigade was probably the most famous Kentucky unit on either side, with the possible exception of Morgan's notorious troopers. Yet the Orphan Brigade's name is more suggestive of the commonwealth's ambiguous role in the struggle than of a Kentucky combat prowess surpassing that of Hoosiers, Hawkeyes, or Tarheels. During their 1862 invasion the Confederate generals Bragg and E. Kirby Smith scathingly agreed that the hearts of Central Kentuckians may have been with the Confederacy, but their heads kept them in the Bluegrass with their horses. The remarks unquestionably tell us more about the disgust of Bragg and Kirby Smith over their inability to recruit fresh troops in Kentucky than about the bravery or cowardice of Kentuckians in the 1860s. Almost certainly the two generals made the typical Confederate mistake of overestimating Kentucky's attachment to the slave states, and underestimating its Unionism. In short, Kentucky's soldiers of the Civil War took a full part in the proceedings, but the day of such famous Kentucky victories as the Battle of the Thames in 1813 was long since past.

For all the returning veterans of the Civil War, peacetime required the collecting of scattered pieces of lives that had been rudely disrupted. For Kentucky, with so many veterans from both sides, the postwar years presented an especially formidable task: healing the scars of fratricidal strife. That task would be hard, but not insurmountable, as was suggested by Valentine H. Stone, an officer of the Federal army, in a poignant assurance to his Rebel brother Henry: "Wherever you go, and whatever you do, you will always carry with you the love and affection of myself."

2

REACHING ABROAD (1865–1918)

DURING the half-century after the Civil War the American armed forces arrived at the threshold of a professional maturity that of course reflected the economic and political modernization which was transforming all of society. By 1917 the United States had reached industrial full bloom; its 1861 population had tripled; and there was an organizational complexity to its governmental and economic structures that would have bewildered earlier generations. Over the same period, what had once been a frontier constabulary evolved into the nucleus of a twentieth-century citizens' army, and a tiny wooden navy became a powerful fleet. The principles of managerial efficiency gained at least a foothold of acceptance in the command systems of the army and navy.

Paralleling the emergence of the United States Navy was the career of Kentucky's Rear Adm. James E. Jouett. The son of the Lexington artist Matthew Jouett, James went to sea at fourteen with a midshipman's appointment from Sen. John J. Crittenden. He boarded his first ship in 1840, when the navy was a force of only eight thousand men and a handful of barnacle-encrusted sailing ships. By the time of his retirement some fifty years later, the navy's steel-plated, steam-powered battlecruisers had become the nation's first line of defense. Jouett's first captain was reputedly the "most cold-blooded martinet in the Navy." Fellow officer-apprentices enjoined young James never to open his mouth while on the ship's quarterdeck except to say "Starboard," "Port," "Yes, sir," and "No, sir." Twenty years later Jouett fought in the Civil War, a conflict in which the navy made a disproportionately large contribution to the Union victory despite having less than 6 percent of all men in service. At the crucial Battle of Mobile Bay in August 1864, Lieutenant Commander Jouett skippered the gunboat *Metacomet*. In perilously shallow waters he captured the *Selma,* whose captain was an old friend; the two shared a dinner of crabs and oysters after the fight. Jouett broke out his admiral's flag in 1884. Within a year he received orders to carry out a typical exercise in late-nineteenth-century gunboat diplomacy. Jouett landed a battalion of marines for the protection of the Panama Railroad from the rampaging local populace. French-owned, the railroad was incorporated in the United States, which enjoyed the guaranteed right of transit across the isthmus under an 1846 treaty. The mere presence of Jouett's naval force calmed the popular passions. The admiral died in 1902, shortly before a Panamanian uprising against Colombia led to the American construction of an isthmian canal.

The profession of arms had definite drawbacks in the nineteenth century. The traditional avenues to commissions were West Point and Annapolis, academies with admission only by congressional appointment. Thus career officers usually came from comparatively well-off—or at least well-connected—families. An officer's life was characterized by low pay, small public esteem, snail's-pace promotion, and duty in remote locales, where temptations were many.

Chapman C. Todd was one officer who saw a promising naval career jeopardized by strong drink. A member of a well-known Kentucky family and an 1866 Naval Academy graduate, Todd took to the bottle apparently while stationed at bleak Sitka, Alaska, in the 1870s. He obtained reinstatement to duty after fourteen months' suspension only by signing a Christian Temperance "Murphy pledge" of abstinence. Except for one lapse Todd seems to have keep his pledge, even though he was subsequently assigned to the most rigorous of sea duty: patrolling the pestilent west coast of Africa. "The climate here is terribly dehibilitating &

few ships remaining here more than a week Escape getting the African fever among their officers and men," he wrote in March 1885 from near the mouth of the Congo. "We were sent . . . to give moral support to our Commissioner, Mr. Tisdal, who went up the Country to see what the chances were for building railroads." Chapman's record continued to haunt him, causing him to be passed over for promotion. "Successful professional work under the most trying circumstances weighs little in the general standing of an officer," he complained. "Some go through life doing next-to-nothing . . . and yet are never touched by the examining Board & going from grade to grade without a question. Many good officers have been forced out of the service by a technicality." Chapman Todd eventually lived down the black mark in his personnel file, retiring as a rear admiral in 1902.

Some officers relished thoroughly the exotic places to which they were sent for the vague purpose of "showing the flag." S.I.M. Major of Versailles, Kentucky, was assigned in 1902 to the U.S.S. *Wilmington* on the China station, which afforded the opportunity to see an ancient and proud empire seemingly destined to be carved up by the great powers into commercial and political spheres of influence. An enthusiastic tourist, Major never dreamed that the turn-of-the-century Western presence in China he vividly described could be so short lived. On a six-hundred-mile cruise up the Yangtze to Hankow, he was pleasantly surprised to find many European residents, "and consequently civilization," in the city of half a million inhabitants. Hankow boasted a "golf club, race course, finely finished clubs, and houses. . . . The missionaries . . . live in great plenty behind their brick walls." Despite their attractions, Chinese cities were "sans exception the filthiest and most ill smelling spots on earth." The naval officers regarded Shanghai as "by far the best place in China" because of that city's "delightful club" of which they were all honorary members: "That is one of the many good things about the Navy—we always receive invitations to all the clubs wherever we go." Major and his messmates employed no fewer than nine Chinese servants—"two laundrymen, steward, cook and five boys." Major's own "valet de chambre," he wrote, was "a cute little 'chink,' with a very solemn face and a shining black que. . . . He is a mind reader when it comes to anticipating wants."

From 1900 the United States maintained an extraterritorial military presence in China to sustain the Open Door policy: an insistence upon equitable access to the country for American missionaries and business entrepreneurs. As late as 1929 William J. Marshall of Henderson, Kentucky, was a junior officer on a gunboat periodically cruising as far as a thousand miles up the Yangtze solely to convey missionaries downstream to the railhead at Nanking. At the time, the Nationalist dictator Chiang Kai-shek controlled only the south bank; semifeudal warloads held the northern shore. Marshall remembers that each time the boat passed a certain bluff it was sprayed with machine-gun fire from the warlords. Fortunately, the guns could not be depressed far enough to strike the boat any lower than three feet from the top of its smokestack. The stack was usually riddled with holes, but the American sailors simply dismissed the harassment as a routine occupational hazard.

During his long naval career, Hugh Rodman of Frankfort, Kentucky, visited most of the globe. An 1880 Annapolis graduate, Rodman was to command as a rear admiral America's World War I battleship squadron in the North Sea. Rodman spent his early career aboard such vessels as the U.S.S. *Hartford,* which had flown Admiral Farragut's flag at New Orleans and Mobile Bay and was a wooden craft that usually operated under sail. Once, Rodman spent 265 days of a year aboard a ship displacing a mere sixteen hundred tons.

Rodman's attitude toward his life's work reflected the outlook of the Old Navy more than the New. He was rather contemptuous of the theoretical training for high command in future wars offered from the mid-1880s by the Naval War College and its renowned professor of naval history, Alfred Thayer Mahan. After all, Mahan "was not a good seaman," Rodman pointed out from personal experience, having been aboard a wooden cruiser commanded by Mahan when it collided with a collier. Admittedly a superb shiphandler himself, the Rodman of World War I was regarded as a military fossil by at least one progressive-minded war-college graduate, the future Fleet Adm. Ernest J. King. But if

Rodman was a self-professed practical seaman—not a theorist, innovator, or reformer—he at least had a keen interest in seamanship, gunnery, marine biology, and the geography and social customs of the countries he visited. He did some advance reading on the history of every port of call. Like so many sailors, Rodman was charmed by the natives of the South Pacific. Once, when he and some companions admired the brightly colored hula skirts of some dancers, they "were surprised to see the coy maidens, after a hurried and almost blushing consultation, doff their skirts, present them to us and beg us to keep them as a momento of the occasion! Moral: Never admire a woman's ball-gown." Rodman shared a general distaste among naval officers for Christian missionaries, although protecting the churchmen partly justified the existence of their service before 1917. Ministers sometimes asked to conduct shipboard worship, a decision Rodman usually referred to his officers and men: "Since a gunboat is a small affair, during service everything else in the ship had to be subordinated to that. It was like an invasion of one's home." Rodman once proposed that his men attend church on shore: "To my surprise and disgust I was informed that such a rough class of men would not be welcome visitors in their midst, the implication being that their presence might contaminate the congregation."

A naval career before 1898 was at least more variegated than one in the army. And Annapolis was less of an ordeal than West Point because the midshipmen could look forward to the annual pleasures of their summer cruises. But both academies were demanding; each subjected its first-year students to hazing that ranged from the trite to the sadistic. Academically, both offered an engineering and practical-military curriculum that rewarded rote learning more than critical and independent study. A sample question on the Military Academy entrance examination at the time that Henry T. Allen of Sharpsburg, Kentucky, took it in 1878 was to "divide 3380321 by MDCCXCIX and express the quotient by the Roman system of notation." If nothing else, a pre-1917 product of West Point or Annapolis was well prepared for active service in the minuscule army or navy of that era, and he had been imbued with a stern sense of personal honor and a simple and lasting commitment to duty.

From the origins of the republic, the perennial mission of the United States Army had been to police the western frontier. Although the tempo of the Indian wars subsided after 1876, some action continued until 1890. George B. Duncan of Lexington, Kentucky, graduated from West Point in June 1886 and reported to the 9th Infantry at Fort Wingate, New Mexico, the next October. In his old age Duncan recalled that "the post trader's store was in full blast. The . . . officers' club was filled night and day and there were card games galore, with stakes from drinks to twenty dollar gold pieces. The bar for enlisted men was lined up until taps. Intoxication was evident on all sides. . . . No military duties were attempted beyond guard mounting and required roll calls." Duncan discovered that his regiment's officers had probably been good soldiers in their day but "had stagnated with inactivity and slow promotion." The regimental commander "was a kindly old gentleman. He wore a full white beard, which fell down to his chest, and he moved on the line of least resistance from his home to his office and back again, carrying a patriarchal staff as an aid to rheumatic joints." Nevertheless, Duncan soon began "to enjoy army life; I had a leisure that business men hoped to attain in their old age, and decided to take my profession seriously and fit myself to its responsibilities."

Even during the slow-moving 1880s and 1890s professional challenges awaited the army officers who sought them. Duncan served for a time as aide to Lt. Gen. John M. Schofield, who had held high command during the Civil War but was nevertheless a forward-looking commanding general of the army from 1888 to 1895. J. Franklin Bell, an 1878 West Point graduate from Shelbyville, Kentucky, and the son of a Confederate captain, developed during twenty years with the 7th Cavalry a consuming interest in unit tactics, and he pioneered the use of the sand table as a teaching device. Hugh L. Scott, a native of Danville, Kentucky, laboriously made himself into the foremost service authority on Indian sign languages. Scott's interest in and sympathy for primitive peoples set him apart from run-of-the-mill members of his calling. In 1885 Henry T. Allen explored some of Alaska's forbidding interior, and four years later wrangled an assignment as the first American military attaché in Russia.

The outbreak of the Spanish-American War in April 1898 removed any pleasure that ambitious officers might have derived from the routine of peacetime soldiering. Historical accounts of 1898 have censured President William McKinley for failing to avoid the war, and the military establishment for mismanaging it. The unreadiness to fight of the army, especially, was almost criminal. Yet the services benefited from a conflict that laid bare such glaring deficiencies in preparedness that few could question the urgent need to undertake a well-conceived series of military reforms after 1901. Fortunately, the Spaniards of 1898 were too inept to take advantage of America's numerous weaknesses.

Excitement, confusion, and boredom marked in more or less equal measure the brief wartime experiences of Kentucky's participants. Using as a core the guardsmen of the state's militia, Kentucky shipped off three regiments of volunteers, but before they had done any real fighting the war had ended. For military careerists the Splendid Little War was a godsend. Aside from Indian campaigns, it was the first opportunity that any American officer under fifty had had to practice his trade. Here was the chance of a lifetime to get recognition and promotion.

From Fort Sheridan, Illinois, George Duncan entrained with the 4th Infantry for Tampa, Florida, where the United States was massing its armed might for a descent upon Cuba and Puerto Rico. Duncan found Tampa to be in chaos. No one in responsibility knew where the dozens of fast-arriving units were to bivouac. Moreover, "the supply departments had fallen down. . . . The single track railroad was unprepared for the demands upon it. . . . No officer of the Subsistence Department . . . had been able to handle the situation. The last one after a day or two had asked to be retired." Munitions and rations began to arrive only after some young, vigorous officers began unsnarling the entanglements of supply and administration that had bedazed their tottering seniors.

Compared to the army, the Spanish-American War navy was a model of smooth efficiency. At the beginning of hostilities, Sam Major was still an Annapolis midshipman. By the end of May, he and his fifty-two classmates had learned that instead of their usual summer cruise they were to spend the next four months on active service with the fleet. In 1898 the sandy peninsula of Florida was a far cry from the bustling vacation mecca of later years. At Key West Sam and five companions "put up at the only hotel in town—at $4 a day. Everything was so crowded that we . . . slept in a room in another part of town, and the mosquitoes, heat, and the thought that I was paying $4 a day with only $15 in my pocket made me miserable." Major finally joined his assigned ship, the U.S.S. *New York,* off Santiago, Cuba, "after four weeks of traveling." By then, while serving temporarily on the *Annapolis,* he had helped to place the army in Cuba. Assigned by his skipper to the command of a steam launch with a crew of five and a one-pound gun in the bow, Major "landed troops from 6 o'clock one morning to six o'clock the next morning, stopping only for meals and fuel. I must have put over a thousand of Uncle Sam's fighters on Cuban soil." Despite a fierce tropical sun which burned Major's nose a "bright scarlet," the American "jackies worked manfully and made a very good job of it." Over the three days required to put ashore twenty thousand soldiers with provisions and horses, only one soldier and five or six horses were lost in the surf. The defending Spaniards had been driven back from the shoreline by naval gunfire. The *Annapolis* lobbed shell after shell at the town of Daiquiri, and Major "watched every shot strike, and one fell right in a column of Spanish soldiers, who scattered in all directions. . . . The army had a little skirmish back in the hills a few days ago. . . . I think they belonged to Roosevelt's Weary Walkers." The soldiers to whom Major referred were of course the fabled Rough Riders of Col. Leonard Wood and Lt. Col. Theodore Roosevelt, a volunteer cavalry regiment of cowboys and collegians whose horses had been left in Florida for lack of shipping space.

By mid-August the fighting in Cuba had ended. More American lives had been lost to yellow fever and malaria than to Spanish bullets. But halfway across the world the United States was about to embark upon a much longer and costlier war than the Caribbean conflict, the subjugation of the Philippine Islands. The outbreak of war with Spain had found Hugh Rodman at Hong Kong with Commodore George Dewey's small Asiatic squadron. Under orders to attack and destroy the Spanish Pacific fleet,

Dewey's ships promptly steamed toward the Philippines. At dark on April 30 Dewey entered Manila Bay. Throughout the night his ships continued to make slow headway in a single column. By dawn, which "comes up like thunder" in the tropics, the ships had reached Manila's waterfront. "To me," Rodman recalled, "the most glorious effect of the whole day occured when we sighted the Spanish fleet at Cavite . . . [and] turned . . . toward it." Dewey's *Olympia* hoisted a signal to engage the enemy, and "immediately the two bands in the fleet began playing 'The Star Spangled Banner,' officers and men alike stood at attention as if on parade, and as the last note died away, simultaneously there came a rousing cheer, and the guns opened on the enemy." Making five runs at ever narrower ranges past the anchored Spaniards, Dewey's Americans shelled the enemy fleet into submission. At one point in the action Rodman was sent below to check on the powder division on his ship, the U.S.S. *Raleigh*: "I heard the sound of a fiddle accompanied by a couple of guitars, and . . . discovered the men . . . strung out across the deck, dressed in abbreviated gunny-sacks to represent *hula* skirts, burlesquing a dance and singing in chorus . . . 'There'll Be a Hot Time in the Old Town To-night.' " President McKinley was dumbstruck to learn that Dewey's fleet had staked an American claim to the Philippines, not having known the precise location of the archipelago. But McKinley recovered quickly enough to demand that the Spaniards cede the islands, an insistence that eventually commited the United States to a long, costly, and extremely nasty guerrilla war against the independence-minded Filipino people.

The suppression of the Philippine Insurrection evoked none of the popular brouhaha accompanying the outbreak of the Spanish-American War. The American people displayed scant interest in the strategic and commercial advantages that acquiring the archipelago was expected to bestow upon the United States. Had there been any intimation of the magnitude of the campaign needed to raise the stars-and-stripes over the distant islands, public sentiment would doubtless have insisted upon either immediate independence for the Philippines or their restoration to Spanish rule. The hostilities that began in February 1899 were by no means over on 4 July 1902 when President Theodore Roosevelt proclaimed the formal close of the insurrection. A total of about a hundred thousand troops eventually fought in what amounted to a colonial war on the far side of the globe. These at first included some National Guard and volunteer units—the latter were raised at large, not by states—but the main burden fell upon a regular army with a post-1901 strength more than twice that of the beginning of 1898. It was in the Philippines that the United States Army crossed the threshold of the twentieth century.

In contrast to his Vietnam War counterpart some six decades later, the typical American soldier of the Philippine Insurrection was less educated and politically sophisticated. He was more apt to have a strong sense of unit loyalty and pride, traits built on long-standing personal relationships. Since field duty in the Philippines was not limited to twelve-month tours, there was not the constant turnover of unit personnel typical of the Vietnam War. Moreover, there were no conscripts in the Philippines. In both conflicts charges abounded that American troops had committed wanton cruelties against innocent natives. In response the Americans demanded to know how they could reasonably be expected to tell ordinary villagers from wily cutthroats. Filipino prisoners under interrogation were sometimes tortured into revealing the whereabouts of guerrillas and hidden caches of weapons. And the Americans resorted on occasion to harsh measures against villages where partisans were harbored. The Philippine Insurrection was not a gentleman's war on either side.

For the Kentuckians George B. Duncan, J. Franklin Bell, and Henry T. Allen, the conflict was a harsh school giving excellent preparation for future responsibilities in high rank. Still with the 4th Infantry, Duncan found, as had so many career soldiers, that the challenge of commanding a company was a major professional milestone. On one early and fruitless sortie out of Manila, his men were continuously in action or on the march for thirty-two hours. Men from other outfits straggled, but Duncan returned to camp with an intact company: "The cooks had coffee and soup ready but had to go around to arouse and feed the men, for they were lying around on the ground in a comatose condition. Bloody socks attested [to] the condition of my feet as a result of this day's work." Encouragement could sometimes help the fainthearted to overcome their fears. Duncan once stopped a hysterical private from raising an alarm that the company's camp was about to be stormed by bolo-wielding guerrillas. Calmly, Duncan directed the man to get his rifle and together they made a careful search of nearby bushes, finding nothing there. The private turned out to be a good soldier who afterward was "grateful that I had never let the story out."

Duncan developed a typical troopleader's distrust of the paper pushers in snug staff billets. While serving as a temporary adjutant he read an elaborate report giving troop locations for every hour of the day, including that of a field-artillery unit, "whose sergeant had told me that he had not fired a shot, and had just wandered around all day trying to find someone to whom to report." Putting down the spurious document, Duncan snorted contemptuously that "war as it's fit is quite different from war as it's writ."

Before the 4th Infantry was shipped home in 1902, Duncan was to lead a battalion and act briefly as regimental commander, but he remained a permanent captain. In contrast, professional lightning struck J. Franklin Bell during his Philippine tour. Having long chafed over his slim prospects for promotion, Bell once calculated that if he stayed in the cavalry he would never go beyond captain before being caught by the army's mandatory retirement age of sixty-four. Accordingly, he transferred into the Judge Advocate General's Corps in 1898, which automatically advanced him from first lieutenant to captain. Soon Maj. Gen. Wesley Merritt took Bell to the Philippines as a temporary staff major. In July 1899 Bell got command of the 36th Volunteer Infantry as a temporary colonel. Out in front of his regiment near Porac, Luzon, on 9 September 1899 he personally charged seven concealed insurgents. Armed with nothing but his officer's pistol, he nevertheless captured three of the Filipinos while still under the fire of the others, a feat which won for him the Medal of Honor. Two months later Bell pinned on the star of a brigadier general of volunteers, although he remained a mere permanent captain. In February 1901, however, when the number of generals' slots increased with the expansion of the regular army, President McKinley nominated Bell for one of the new brigadiers' vacancies, a promotion for merit which leapfrogged him over 1,036 officers previously ahead of him on the seniority list. At the time of his promotion Bell was the army's 585th captain. Only forty-five years old in 1901, he was assured of a bright professional future.

Undoubtedly, Frank Bell sensed the jealousy of those left in his wake. As chief-of-staff of the army from 1906 to 1910, he was loathe to allow other meritorious officers to bypass the established pecking order as he had. A particularly noteworthy victim of Bell's new-found devotion to the seniority system was his fellow Kentuckian and cavalryman Henry T. Allen. As a thirty-nine-year-old first lieutenant (and major of volunteers) Allen had in Cuba his very first chance to lead men in action. Sent on to the Philippines in 1899, he was placed in charge of the newly formed Philippine Constabulary in 1901, which gave him the pay and prerogatives, and subsequently the temporary rank, of brigadier general. Allen's organization acted as a semi-military native police force. He selected his American officers carefully, demanding youthful, brave, and physically tough individuals. Convinced that boozers would be of little value in keeping the peace, Allen pointedly inquired of each officer applicant to the constabulary whether he was a drinker. He did accept one man who asserted that "I drink all I want, and any time I want. But . . . drunk or sober, I can fight like hell!" Allen also insisted that his Filipino recruits be recommended by two native leaders but made an exception of one volunteer who brought in, as promised, the heads of an insurrectionary chief and several of his followers. The Philippine Constabulary drew down the wrath of such prominent army officers as Maj. Gen Arthur MacArthur, who vehemently railed against the efforts of William Howard Taft, head of the Philippine Commission, to establish civil government over the island at the earliest possible date. Unfortunately, Allen's overbearing ways also peeved Taft, who was to be secretary of war when Bell became chief-of-staff.

Early in 1907 Allen sought General Bell's support for his quest to get his temporary star made permanent. Allen's biographer has shown that from 1902 to 1906 Allen's constabulary had had an average strength of 6,400 men, compared to some 17,000 in the army's Philippine contingent. During that period the constabulary lost 971 men killed as opposed to only 239 for the army. Thus for some five years Allen's command carried the main burden of pacifying the islands, and Allen held one of the most vital assignments in the army. In view of the precedent established by the extraordinary promotions of Bell and several other officers, Allen's urgings on his own behalf do not seem unreasonable. But Bell shattered his hopes. Within months Allen was back in his permanent grade of major and was exercising command of 5 officers and 129 men at Yellowstone National Park. Ten years had passed before he was again a general officer.

Whatever Allen may have felt after 1907 about his erstwhile friend, J. Franklin Bell was an effective chief-of-staff. The office was new, dating back only to 1903. Before then the army's commanding general, usually its senior general, normally served until death or retirement. No commanding general in recent memory had done much commanding. Instead, the army was largely run by the chiefs of the respective staff bureaus, officers who were entrenched in Washington with permanent tenure and dealt directly with the secretary of war and Congress. The bureau heads kept the War Department thoroughly enmeshed in the red tape of day-to-day political and administrative routine. Within the army there had long been proponents of abolishing the office of commanding general and establishing a new general staff to coordinate the bureaus and develop plans for all imaginable contingencies. Its chief would not command directly but would be the principal military advisor of the president and secretary of war. War Department chaos in 1898 under Secretary Russell A. Alger and Maj. Gen. Nelson A. Miles lent urgency to the reform proposals, and Secretary of War Elihu Root pushed the needed legislation through Congress in 1903. The fourth chief-of-staff, Bell was the first to be selected ahead of senior, but less suitable, officers.

During Bell's four-year tour, he improved the readiness of a profoundly conservative military establishment in several ways. Disdaining in promotion policy the spectacular defiance of age and tradition that had advanced him, Bell at least urged that merit be the primary consideration in selecting colonels for brigadier general. Several European armies practiced "plucking," an up-or-out pattern of promotion or early retirement, but Bell concluded that Congress would reject the concept because of the additional expense in pension payments that it would entail, and that the resultant defeat would weaken the General Staff in its struggle with the bureaus for primacy in the War Department.

The most formidable roadblock in the way of Bell's professional supremacy within the service was Fred Ainsworth, the adjutant general. Ainsworth had no program of his own for army development, but he was a master bureaucrat who guarded jealously the prerogatives of his office. As custodian of the army's records, Ainsworth was uniquely positioned to oblige congressmen with inquiries from their constituents about military pensions. From his long years there, Ainsworth grasped the political nuances of the capital as Bell—who had spent most of his career in the field—never could. Lacking in Taft a dynamic secretary of war, Bell chose not to force a crisis with Ainsworth. But his successor, Maj. Gen. Leonard Wood, did so in 1912 with the firm backing of Secretary of War Henry L. Stimson; Ainsworth was forced into retirement.

To the army Bell emphasized that its peacetime mission was preparation for war. Military education made noteworthy gains during his term of office. The line and technical branches developed professional schools, and the Command and General Staff School at Fort Leavenworth, Kansas, came of age. Bell himself had headed the school before becoming chief-of-staff, and his biographer writes that during "World War I the Leavenworth graduates provided a critical nucleus of highly trained professionals who filled the key staff slots at Chaumont [the high command] and army, corps, and division headquarters."

Before the end of his term as chief-of-staff Frank Bell discovered that he had diabetes. After 1910 he nevertheless held other important commands, but age and ill health kept him in the United States during the Great War. The 77th Infantry Division, which he had trained, sailed without him. The fates were kinder to George Duncan, Henry Allen, and Hugh Rodman. For these officers, as well as thousands of less-prominent Kentuckians, there were opportunities to be grasped and stern tests to be faced "over there."

The First World War was well into its third year when America joined the fray on 6 April 1917. Since late 1914 the major nations of Europe had been stalemated in the mud and barbed wire of such far-flung battlefields as the Marne, Verdun, and Gallipoli. By the hundreds of thousands their young men had been slaughtered by unprecedentedly lethal weapons: automatic rifles, machine guns, howitzers, and poison gas.

The magnitude of America's war effort of 1917–18 was amazing. Armistice Day intervened before the country's industrial buildup had reached its full stride, but there was no reason to doubt that American war production would have been spectacular had the conflict continued into 1919. More importantly, in a span of just over eighteen months the nation placed more than four million citizens under arms and shipped some two million overseas. Most of the American doughboys served on the Western Front, a continuous line of trenches running from the English Channel to the Swiss border. The mobilization was especially impressive because as recently as June 1916 the American armed forces had numbered a mere 179,000 men. Regulars, volunteers, and National Guard militiamen provided a respectable share of the World War I manpower, but for the first time in history a majority of America's fighting men were draftees. The Civil War was the only previous instance of an American draft, although conscription had filled the ranks of many European armies since the Napoleonic wars. From across the United States in 1917–18 no fewer than 2.8 million men were inducted; Kentucky furnished 57,569 draftees. An additional 26,603 Kentuckians entered the army as volunteers, while still others served in the navy or Marine Corps. Kentucky-born Maj. Gen. Hugh L. Scott had laid the groundwork for the federal draft act of May 1917. The army's chief-of-staff until he retired in September 1917, Scott had urged in his annual report for 1916 that the volunteer system be relegated to the past. The only democratic way to raise an army, he declared, was national imposition of a universal obligation to serve in wartime. Although President Woodrow Wilson had previously balked at demands for the draft from his partisan Republican critics Theodore Roosevelt and Maj. Gen. Leonard Wood, he was sufficiently impressed by Scott's logic to direct that Secretary of War Newton D. Baker have a conscription bill readied for submission to Congress.

War with Germany brought such volunteers as B. F. Dawes of Cynthiana, Kentucky. To the army's recruiters, the seventy-year-old Dawes wrote that he was "pretty active for my age, [and] would like to help my country in some way. . . . Never was married and have no strings on me to keep me at home. Would love to put the Kaiser and his military autocracy out of commission." Dawes offered to serve as a cook, provided that "if we get into a fight the United States will furnish me with a gun and ammunition while the fight lasts or as long as I last." But the American armed forces of 1917–18 had no place for men of Dawes's age.

During the weeks and months after April 1917 thousands of draftees from Kentucky, Indiana, and Illinois poured into Camp Taylor, near Louisville, for basic training. Among them was Michael A. Lewis, one of about fifty young men to answer the roll in front of the Hardin County courthouse on the bright morning of 23 February 1918. Following dinner at the Smith Hotel, they traveled by troop train to Camp Taylor, where each man was "issued three blankets, one bed sack & etc." After "awkwardly" eating their first meal from army messkits, the new inductees "crept silently to bed." Lewis "did not go to sleep for some time and I shall never forget how lonely I felt when taps were sounded."

Few of the trainees at Camp Taylor had either time or energy to fret over a disturbingly high rate of rejections on army preinduction physical examinations administered in Kentucky. The recruits were much more concerned over wretched training conditions at Taylor. In December 1917 the *Louisville Herald* reported that "the camp yesterday was little short of a huge sea of mud. The drill grounds were transformed into swamps and pools of water, some of them as large as ponds. . . . To walk a distance of ten yards without sinking ankle-deep into mud was impossible."

In contrast to the popularly elected junior officers of 1861–65, World War I leaders were chosen with some care by the War Department. Besides the hard core of professionals, officers came from the National Guard, where during recent years they had had to meet minimum physical and professional standards to qualify for "federal recognition." Moreover, male graduates of such land-grant institutions as the University of Kentucky had usually undergone two or more years of rudimentary military training while in school. Then, too, there were college, business, and professional men who had voluntarily attended army summer camps held in a variety of locales between 1913 and 1916 to impart at least the basics of military leadership. All of the participants were called Plattsburgers, after the New York encampment that drew men from Wall Street and the Ivy League.

From May 1917 Plattsburgers and numerous others passed through three months of officer-candidate training before pinning on their gold bars as second lieutenants. Army old-timers derided the new officers, calling them ninety-day wonders. Nevertheless, the ninety-day men were better prepared than the volunteer officers of any previous American war. A remarkably untypical Plattsburg alumnus and officer-candidate was Samuel M. Wilson, a forty-three-year-old Lexington attorney. Upon the declaration of war Wilson exerted every influence to get himself commissioned. His uncle, General Frank Bell, made the necessary arrangements. Wilson had hardly begun his officer-candidate course before his company commander "discovered that he was afflicted with deafness of such a serious nature as to disqualify him for duty in the line." Nevertheless, Wilson swiftly rose to lieutenant colonel and judge advocate of the 77th Infantry Division, thanks to the unwavering support of Bell. To Judge Advocate General Enoch Crowder in Washington, Bell had written that he was "exceedingly anxious to get this appointment" for Wilson, and was prepared in turn to endorse Crowder "for any appointment you might want."

Wilson's friend and fellow Bluegrass lawyer, Clinton Harbison, found his officer-candidate course at Fort Benjamin Harrison, Indiana, to be "strenuous." Harbison was "very much impressed with the thoroughness of our training. . . . There is an undertone of seriousness about it that makes you feel like giving up everything else in the world." The War Department prescribed the curriculum "down to the details of the number of hours to be devoted to each subject." There was "less actual physical exercise than at Plattsburg . . . but a great deal of every day is taken up with conference and study."

Normally, young men make better soldiers than those who are already established in civilian pursuits. A youthful sense of optimism and eagerness for adventure can ease the sometimes painful adjustment to new faces and surroundings. His enthusiasm for flight training at Dayton, Ohio, carried Victor H. Strahm of Bowling Green, Kentucky, buoyantly through the vexations of army life: "We have to be in bed at 11 o'clock. Have to march to all classes and have to air our bed out every day. Also lots of others [rules] which are fine for us." The time eventually came for about half of the Americans in uniform to depart for the war zones of Europe. A native of Calloway County, Kentucky, Sgt. Felix C. Holt crossed the United States by troop train from Camp Kearny, California: "Have had one grand time since we left Kearny, for we have had music and singing all the way. Also the eats have been good, so there is no kick coming from me so far. . . . The people along the way sure have been good to us. At one town last night they gave us a lot of stuff to eat and . . . about 40 good-looking damsels sang for us."

Although crowded, shipboard conditions on the ocean liners used as troop transports for the long voyage to France were reasonably comfortable, especially for officers. With little to do, Lt. Howard Kinne of Stearns, Kentucky, passed his ten days at sea with games of chess. Victor Strahm had a "wonderful time," writing that "our food has been fine all the way, . . . roast chicken, turkey or duck every day, also meats, all kinds of fruits, eggs and everything we could want." His ship had joined its convoy at Halifax, Nova Scotia, where "the British battleships played patriotic songs, and as we passed them on our way to the sea they lowered their flags to half mast and played the 'star-spangled banner.' It sure thrilled us and aided our desired to be over there." Inside the U-boat zone lifejackets had to be worn at all times, but Strahm thought that the German submarines must be "a little scared of us, 'cause we are well-armed and are also convoyed by a big bunch of destroyers which look like they could cause a lot of trouble."

Landing in France, Felix Holt's outfit, the 115th Field Signal Battalion, traveled "via the Box Car Route" for forty-eight hours, then undertook "a nine mile hike with a 50 lb pack, and it rained while we were on the march." Holt's battalion set up shop in "a quaint little village." The culture shock that so often accompanies foreign travel made the Kentucky Yanks of 1917–18 especially aware that France was an old and hauntingly beautiful country. "Everything is new and strange to me and it is very interesting," Holt recorded. "The People have treated us royally everywhere in France, and though I can talk very little French I can make myself fairly well understood. The French kids are very generous with their time, for they spend it all with us teaching us the lingo. Also the young damsels do their share and I must say there are some swell lookers here. . . . There are a couple of them visiting here from Paris and B-LE-ME they are sure some dames."

The vanguard of the more than two million American troops eventually sent to France was the 1st Division, the 26th Infantry Regiment of which was headed by George Duncan, now a colonel. At the French village where Duncan established regimental headquarters, the mayor and schoolchildren greeted the Americans with oratory and flowers. Duncan's usual French interpreter was away, "so I took a Canadian Frenchman to translate what I had to say—just a few words—but the soldier launched into a panegeric, and I pulled him off the steps when I heard the words 'LaFayette' and 'Rochambeau.' But all responded to his effort with applause. I never knew just what he said." A subsequent visitor to the regiment was the venerable political leader Georges Clemenceau, known as the Tiger of France. In fluent English, Clemenceau assured the Americans that "they represented a country that had lighted the beacon of liberty as an inspiration to every nation of the world, and that now they were again leading the way to see that liberty did not perish from the earth."

If the exuberant doughboys of 1917–18 appear foolishly naive to modern eyes, and if the warmth of their welcome to France is hard to believe, it must be remembered that six decades ago the United States was a newcomer to the alliances and wars of Europe. To the British and French alike the coming of the New World to the battles of the Old offered a last hope of eventual escape from the horrors of war in the trenches. Samuel Wilson's Kentucky friend Lt. Horace M. Gray understood perfectly the attitude of the French toward their new comrades in arms: "The French treat us as well as anyone could dream of, and act as though they couldn't do enough. The general feeling is that our coming will greatly shorten the war and will make victory certain. It also appears to them that we have considered both sides of the question and have decided that they are fighting for the right and have come to add our might to theirs."

Months went by before any American troops fought in northeastern France. The flow across the Atlantic of American manpower began in the first weeks after the American declaration of war, but the doughboys needed hardening for battle after their arrival in Europe. Moreover, the American commander, Gen. John J. Pershing, was adamant that his men were not to be frittered away in company- and battalion-sized lots as replacements in the exhausted and disillusioned ranks of the British and French. When his Yanks entered the fight, Pershing vowed, they would do so as divisions, corps, and field armies, and they would be trained to sustain a successful offensive—not merely to continue the stationary trench-warfare bloodletting of the dreary months since late 1914. To achieve his goals Pershing established innumerable training programs and schools of military instruction. Horace Gray, for example, practiced gunnery and horsemanship at the field artillery school. "Every day," he wrote, "we have equitation with French Dragoon officers as instructors. We have a riding hall with a tan bark floor, and it is really a pleasure to fall off if one does it right. I have done it right every time but once. We have French saddles with no stirrups so that we will get our 'seat.' About half of my section are in the liniment stage." True to the traditions of the Bluegrass, Gray did not pause to wonder why an artillery officer needed to be an expert horseman in a war that was crushing out the last vestiges of the age of chivalry.

Months before American units went into battle, their officers were touring the French combat sector. They were unceasingly scrutinized by a stream of staff officers from Chaumont, where Pershing had located his headquarters. The commanding general was swift to relieve any officer found deficient by his staff. Moreover, a number of major generals visited France in advance of their divisions, giving Pershing the opportunity to assess them in person. If he occasionally treated a commander unfairly, there were others he was right to "pluck." He rejected J. Franklin Bell on grounds of age and health. Brokenhearted, Bell died in 1919. Passing muster, however, was Henry T. Allen, who at fifty-eight was older than Pershing and had been senior to him before Pershing jumped from captain to brigadier in 1906. Allen had won Pershing's confidence in 1916 by bearing up under the pounding of a four-hundred-mile horseback pursuit of Pancho Villa's Mexican guerrillas. George Duncan noted that some "older officers" regarded their advance visit to France as if it were "just a sightseeing tour." Duncan himself inherited the 77th Division from the displaced Bell, only to lose it some weeks later. He departed for Blois, Pershing's screening and reassignment purgatory for displaced officers. Some of Duncan's tactical dispositions with the 77th Division had drawn the disfavor of Pershing's staff, but the Iron Commander rated his West Point classmate from Kentucky as "a fighter," his highest praise, and at the beginning of October 1918 he gave Duncan command of the 82d Division.

By July 1918 a million American troops were in France; that number doubled before the November armistice. Arriving in midsummer was Henry Allen's 90th Division, a "national army" outfit composed of Texas and Oklahoma draftees calling themselves the Tough 'Ombres. Not arriving until October was the 38th Division, which had been formed from the National Guard organizations of Kentucky, Indiana, and West Virginia, and which never fought as a division. Its men were fed into other units as replacements. A similar fate befell the national-army 84th Division, filled with many of the Ohio Valley inductees from Camp Taylor.

More and more doughboy divisions entered the fighting as the summer of 1918 advanced, and in late August the First Army finally became operational under Pershing's direct command. In mid-September the new army undertook its first general offensive at Saint-Mihiel. Then on September 26 it grappled with the Germans in the Argonne Forest, a climactic battle of attrition that lasted until November and dwarfed such titanic American bloodlettings of the past as Shiloh and Chickamauga. It was there that German automatic weapons, artillery, and mustard gas inflicted most of the more than 50,000 American battle deaths of the war, including 890 from Kentucky. (Few doughboys would have been aware that Confederate D. R. Williams of Covington, Kentucky, had introduced a primitive machine gun to the battlefields of the world back in 1862.)

Just behind the forward troops in the immense Argonne battle was Pvt. Michael A. Lewis, who had come overseas with the 1st Pioneer Infantry Regiment. Lewis recorded in his diary that at one o'clock in the morning of September 26 "the 72-hour barrage began, opening the big drive. The regiment assembled at 4:30 A.M. to go to the front under heavy shellfire to take charge of the roads leading to the firing line. We marched . . . 8 miles almost . . . as the steady roar all along the roadside came from the artillery. . . . At a large hill . . . [we] could see the waves [of infantry] advancing." Serving as road guards, Lewis's outfit did its "utmost to keep traffic moving." A couple of days later he and his compatriots reverted to their normal duties as combat engineers: "We are building a road across [what was, until recently,] No Man's Land, working both night and day. We have lost so much sleep and have had so little to eat that we are almost worn out." In mid-October the pioneers continued to repair roads, which were generally "in a terrible condition. It has been raining most every day and sometimes we have to scrape the mud and water from the roads."

American noncombat deaths in World War I (including 2,418 from Kentucky) surpassed those of the battlefield—this despite food and medicine much superior to the standards of the Civil War. A principal cause of nonbattle mortalities was a raging influenza epidemic that swept the earth at the close of the Great War, remorselessly killing soldiers and civilians alike. Although bested by the flu, army medical officers did wage a victorious campaign against venereal disease, a scourge of military forces throughout recorded history. French prostitutes (and acquiescent civic officials) were shocked by the stringent patrolling of red-light districts by highhanded American doctors and military police.

For every 1917-18 Yank who died, about two more suffered wounds, and others became temporarily sick or were reported missing. Illness did not respect otherwise safe rear areas, but wounds and straggling gnawed away mainly at a division's "fighting effectives," the comparatively small proportion of its men who were actually front-line soldiers. On 25 October 1918, for instance, George Duncan's 82d Division counted only 3,164 "men actually with weapons in their hands engaged in fighting the enemy" under the direction of 107 platoon leaders. The 82d's authorized strength was 27,082, a total increased by nondivisional support troops to nearly 40,000 men. To keep losses among his fighting effectives from eroding his entire command's fitness for battle, Duncan had to hold down straggling and evacuation, "the two most prolific causes of losses." The division's military police combated straggling by patrolling all likely rear-area hiding places. Losses by evacuation were cut by a careful screening out of men whose wounds or inhalation of poison gas were slight enough to permit treatment and recovery at the division's own field hospital and rest camp. No soldier for whom the doctors foresaw recovery within two weeks was sent any farther to the rear. The hazards and spiritual anguish of battle eventually bring all men to a breaking point. To boost morale Duncan paid ceaseless attention to such details as the regular rotation of battalions in and out of the front line and fresh clothing, hot food, baths, and adequate shelter for the men who were out of the trenches. In keeping with the tone set by the severe Pershing, Duncan confronted individual psychoneurotic disorders with a flinty stare. He directed the divisional psychiatrist "to keep neurological cases near the front, near the sound of the guns, and subjected to long-range artillery fire and air bombardment, as experiments [had] demonstrated that men recovered much more quickly under these conditions than further to the rear . . . and [under] constant coddling." Duncan's treatment of emotional breakdown on the battlefield appears exceedingly harsh in comparison to the much more sympathetic approach taken in later American wars toward what became known as combat fatigue. But Duncan gained considerable success from his labors to maintain the battleworthiness of his division; during one calm eight-day stretch late in October his combat effectives increased by 512, although he received no replacements. Despite the 82d Division's comparatively late entry into combat, it had no fewer than thirty days of battle before the armistice. The price was high: 1,413 men killed and 6,664 wounded.

Other divisions saw even more action than the 82d, but one of Duncan's brigades managed to participate in perhaps the most storied action of the war: the release of the famed "lost battalion" of the 77th from a trap inside the German lines. The exploit involved organizing and executing on extremely short notice an attack that exposed a flank of the 164th Brigade to enfilading German fire. On October 8, the second day of the action, Cpl. Alvin C. York of Tennessee "fearlessly" led seven men into the German lines. A comparatively unsophisticated countryman who had been drafted despite being a conscientious objector, York captured no fewer than 132 Germans and killed others. Asked by Duncan just how he had accomplished his famous feat, York responded that his "father always told me if you get into a scrimmage keep cool and you are sure to get the drop on the other fellow." He added, "General, I would hate to think I missed any of them shots; they were all at pretty close range—50 or 60 yards"!

Certain Kentuckians displayed battlefield gallantry as remarkable as York's, although their deeds were not to be similarly commemorated on the silver screen. The 33d Division's Sgt. Willie Sandlin, whose mountaineer upbringing in Leslie County was akin to that of the Tennesseean, on 26 September 1918 set a "splendid example of bravery and coolness to his men" at Bois-de-Forges. Out in front of his squad, Sandlin wiped out the crew of a machine-gun nest with a grenade, and later that day he twice again made successful single-handed attacks on German machine gunners. Internal damage from poison gas was the attributed cause of Sandlin's relatively early death in 1949, before he had reached his sixtieth birthday.

Over in the 5th Division was Samuel Woodfill, a regular-army sergeant currently in command of a company as a temporary officer. A Hoosier by birth, Woodfill had spent his boyhood in Kentucky, and his wife Blossom passed the war years working a farm near Fort Thomas. Sent forward on October 12 as part of a battalion-scale probe of the German main line, the *Kriemhilde Stellung*, Woodfill and his company encountered automatic-weapon fire from three directions: the loft of an old barn to the left, a brush-concealed pit directly ahead, and a church tower to the right. Taking cover in a shell hole that still reeked of mustard gas, Woodfill with his Springfield rifle picked off in turn each of the Germans in the tower. He did not waste a round although he had to fire at unseen targets two hundred yards away; he calculated his shots by the German Spandau machine gun's muzzle flashes. Next, Woodfill in similar fashion killed a single German firing a light automatic from the barn loft. Then, threading his way from shell hole to shell hole, he picked off the five-man crew of the center machine gun. With his officer's pistol he killed another German, only to be challenged by a Luger-wielding German lieutenant who had been feigning death; Woodfill shot the man through the heart. Before he was finished, Woodfill had picked off the crews of two more machine guns, and having forced his way into the *Kriemhilde Stellung* killed still two other Germans with a pickax. Woodfill's nearly unbelievable demonstration of Old Army markmanship and courage went for naught; with the surviving members of his company he was ordered back to the American line. Shortly, he became deathly ill from pneumonia, to which he had been made vulnerable by poison gas. General Pershing considered Woodfill to be the greatest individual hero of the American Expeditionary Force, and like Sandlin and York he won the Medal of Honor. After the war Woodfill reverted to sergeant.

Civil War combat had portended many aspects of the struggle in the trenches. High above the muddy battlefields, however, military aviation was now adding an entirely new dimension to warfare. The Great War erupted only eleven years after the dawning of the age of powered flight. Understandably, it took some time for the military and political leaders of both sides to grasp the potential of air power. But well before America entered the conflict, the war in the air had captured the imagination of the whole world. The aviators bombed, reconnoitered enemy dispositions, strafed ground troops, and dueled each other in the air. Their individual heroics enshrouded them in a romantic haze.

The American Expeditionary Force took to the air with zest. There were some seventy-three American aces, Victor Strahm among them, with five or more German planes downed. The son of a German-born music professor at the institution known later as Western Kentucky University, Straham was a natural at the lethal game of air combat. He would never have lasted through more than 130 hours of flying behind the German lines had he not been endowed with an exceptional combination of aggressiveness, courage, calculating judgment, and hand-and-eye coordination. Strahm harbored no illusions about his own chances for survival, yet he clearly relished his role in the war. "I am now. *Capt.* Victor H. Strahm, with 4 official Boche and the happiest boy in the world. . . . I had rather fight a Fokker than have the dentist grind on me," he boasted to his worried parents. With boyish enthusiasm he described his assignment with the 91st Aero Squadron: "My duty is long-range reconnaissance into Germany. I do not hunt other planes but let them hunt me, and if they attack me, will I fight. And we can put up a very good fight because we carry 3 machine guns." "Photographing and bombing" as far as "30 and 40 kilometers back into Germany" was both "exciting" and risky. Over Diederhofen, Germany, Vic drove off three attacking German triplanes, and "got quite a few machine-gun bullets in my plane. . . . One bullet went by my hand with which I was controlling the machine and missed it only 2 inches, coming between my legs. . . . It went out through my upper wing. I could see it because it was a tracer and left a little streak of white flame." On 4 September 1918 Strahm led a flight of four planes over the fortress-town of Metz, on the Franco-German border, where they were attacked by eleven Germans. The Americans formed a tight inside circle until Vic "caught an opening, finally, and started out . . . for home, the others following in perfect order." Strahm's flight survived the ten-minute action without loss, and claimed the downing of two German planes.

Among air combatants a studied courtesy was practiced that would have been quite out of place in the trenches. When two men from Strahm's squadron failed to return from a mission, the 91st dropped a note of inquiry inside the German lines. One day later "the Germans dropped us a note . . . telling us the two fellows . . . were prisoners unwounded in their hands. It was very sportsmanlike of them, but then . . . there is always more of the sport & game side of war in flying than in any other branch." Only in the next war would the far-ranging and indiscriminate destructiveness of air warfare be fully manifested.

Enemy fire was not the only hazard faced by American fliers. There was the "Army itch" to contend with on the ground. "It is on our legs and all we do is sit up and scratch all day long," reported Vic. "The doctors suppose that it is a ground microbe common to France."

The off-duty existence of airmen has always been the envy of men in the trenches. As Strahm reported, female canteen workers "do a wonderful work and also have a great time. They were out to entertain us the other night and the Major, myself, and another pilot rode them in our Cadillac for quite a while afterwords." McCreary County's Lt. Howard Kinne, who had quarterbacked the University of Kentucky's football team, was another airman to enjoy life behind the lines: "Every evening after dinner, myself and another officer go to town and play tennis with 2 girls. . . . Their mother is with them all the time, of course, and does most of the talking, but we must pay the price of being with nice girls."

Coming as he did from a family of some local prominence, Howard hoped that a good military record might be of service to him in postwar Kentucky politics. He sensed, however, that as an observer (a photographer and machine gunner in a two-seater aircraft) he was unlikely to win the laurels that would come to a "chase" pilot. The news of the successes won by Victor Strahm (just an ordinary student at the time Kinne had been an athletic and social front-runner at the University of Kentucky) annoyed Kinne considerably. Howard realized that a spectacular future lay in store for aviation. "I am anxious to learn to fly, as aeroplanes are going to be great things from now on," he wrote shortly after leaving the Coast Artillery Corps for training as an observer. In ten years planes "will be cheaper than Fords and everyone will know how to fly."

But from the beginning of his training in aviation, Kinne started to consider the distinct possibility of his own death in the air. "We have lots of fun kidding each other about getting killed and how long we will last," he wrote bravely. "It may sound painful to you but we all expect to live thru it altho of course we don't think much about it." In March 1918 he touched the same chord: "I like . . . [flying] real well and I really don't think of it as very dangerous. . . . It is just a question of who is unlucky or [of] one's resourcefulness." "The chances are 100 to 1 that you will get thru O.K.," he declared in June. From the 99th Aero Squadron to which he had been posted, Kinne noted in August that "2 of the 14 I finished school with over here are thru with the war. One killed and one a prisoner." Death reached very close just one month later: "One of my best friends over here . . . [was] killed by the Boche. . . . I figure I owe the bloody devils one for that, and if I ever get a boche it will be for him. An observer doesn't pick a fight tho, and I will probably never get a boche, as very few observers ever do." On September 14 "we lost an observer. . . . I flew over his grave this AM and dropped some flowers. Seems like they always get the best and leave us scrubs."

Howard Kinne's last letter is dated 22 September 1918: "I have been doing quite a bit of work lately and will have some great stories to tell when I get home. Thus is sure great sport and I like it fine. One of my machine guns is no. 13 and I got a machine-gun bullet right thru it the other day. I don't know whether that is lucky or not." It was not. Exactly seven days later, Howard and his pilot, a Lieutenant McElroy, took off on an evening reconnaissance flight from which they did not return.

In the air and on the ground the American Expeditionary Force was in full offensive swing by 11 November 1918, when an armistice abruptly terminated the war. Had it lasted another year Pershing's men would have shouldered the main burden of an Allied push to the Rhine and beyond. For now, however, the Germans were too exhausted to continue the fight. News of the impending armistice reached Michael Lewis on November 10: "Tonight I went to the fields and prayed alone that it might be signed." The next morning Lewis and his fellow pioneers learned that "the armistice is signed and firing will cease at 11:A.M. The boys shouted for joy. I knew my prayer had been answered. I cried because I was so glad it was all over. Just then we could hear the roar of the guns and as we hiked . . . we heard the last big roar die away and the world seemed quiet. The boys are so happy and every one seems to take life anew."

The tasks of some Kentucky participants in World War I were

not done at the eleventh hour of the eleventh day of the eleventh month of 1918, when the guns went silent. At Sarisbury Court, a massive three-story Tudor manor house near Southampton, England, the doctors and nurses of Base Hospital No. 40 patched and healed bodies maimed in battle. The organizer and chief surgeon of the unit was Maj. David Barrow of Lexington's Good Samaritan Hospital. Most of its 372-person staff were Central Kentuckians, some of whom came from the cream of Bluegrass society. The son of a prominent horse breeder, Louis Haggin was "a five million dollar sergeant." The wealthy John McCormack, who weighed 250 pounds and had consequently needed special permission to enlist, was the Barrow hospital's chief cook. Dr. Barrow and his citizen-soldier medical colleagues derived professional stimulation from their tour of service, but were nonplussed by what they saw of the regular-army physicians, many of whom Barrow labeled as "medical ignoramuses, absolutely devoid of scientific attainment. Familiar with the paper work and red tape of the army, it seemed a joy to them to humiliate the volunteer doctor who was absolutely ignorant of army methods." Barrow also considered the "so-called inspectors" sent down from London to check his patients for cooties to be a first-class nuisance.

Over in France General Henry Allen was present in the Hall of Mirrors at Versailles on 28 June 1919, when German's representatives signed a treaty with provisions for his next assignment: command of the ten-thousand-man occupation of part of the German Rhineland. Within a fortnight Allen arrived at Coblenz to take over the American Forces in Germany from Maj. Gen. Joseph T. Dickman. Once Pershing departed for home in September 1919, Allen's command comprised the American military presence in the Old World. Pershing regarded the Kentuckian as "exactly the right man in the right place" because of the suave Allen's long experience with European protocol as an attaché. Throughout his nearly four years at Coblenz Allen adamantly refused to allow his men to slacken into soft garrison troops. He drove them through rigorous field training, spit-and-polish parade-ground drills, and an extensive educational program emphasizing vocational skills as well as the academic basics. In the spring of 1920 Allen also took a seat on the Interallied Rhineland High Commission. Outside of the chief-of-staff's post, which went to Pershing in 1921, Allen's assignment was probably the most challenging and enjoyable in the postwar army.

Allen's occupation troops were mostly postwar recruits, the doughboys having left France by divisions in the same order that they arrived. Pershing's armies had done most of their fighting in the southern sector of the Western Front, since that was the area most easily supplied from the French Bay of Biscay ports allocated to the American Expeditionary Force. Without ample logistical support it would have been impossible to ship the combat men forward, feed and supply them at the front, and embark them for home once the fighting was done. The armistice threw into reverse gear a mammoth Services of Supply organization. Performing "the hardest kind of labor" at Bordeaux's Bassans docks were the black pioneer infantrymen of a battalion commanded by Maj. Austin Kinniard, a peacetime Louisville businessman. Although the battle zone was hundreds of miles away, Kinniard found it a vexing task to maintain a harmonious, well-disciplined command. The firm but fair-minded major was quick to take umbrage over harassment of his men by officious military police. To his diary Kinniard confided that "the colored soldier is not getting a square deal, in my opinion, in this Base." The Criminal Investigation Bureau was eager for convictions, "regardless of guilt or innocence." Candy and food were planted to entrap the Negroes who stole them. By means of "Third Degree" interrogations "men are made to confess and then tried with no other evidence. At the trial it's impossible to bring out the '3rd Degree' methods, as the J[udge] A[dvocate] absolutely dominates the court, and he pretends to believe that no uncivilized methods are used." Kinniard's Negroes did not find life at Bordeaux entirely unpleasant, however. In February 1919 the major discovered that the comely French waitresses at the Bordeaux officers' club "apparently prefer the colored stevedores to the white officers. There is a saying that they consort with the . . . white enlisted men for car fare, white officers for a living, and the stevedores for pleasure."

Not in length, numbers engaged, nor cost in lives had World War I matched the pain inflicted by the Civil War upon the people of Kentucky. Even though the Battle of the Argonne

Forest far transcended in horror the struggle at Perryville, the fact that it took place thousands of miles from the Bluegrass State inevitably softened its impact. The vast distance between the men "over there" and their families at home meant that the Great War was less of a generally shared experience than the Civil War. Nor was it as much of a collective undertaking for Kentucky's direct participants, individually scattered as they were throughout the American Expeditionary Force, rather than being gathered in locally recruited volunteer regiments.

The First World War did not confront the people of Kentucky with the agony of divided loyalties. If the state of 1861–65 had suffered social lesions requiring half a century to heal, the commonwealth of 1917–18 stood relatively united behind President Wilson's Great Crusade. Yet the aftermath of World War I was to bring national changes as dramatic and sweeping as those following the Civil War. Despite a widespread poignant longing for prewar "normalcy," America was to pass in dizzying succession through the Roaring Twenties, the Great Depression, and the Second World War.

Mercifully, perhaps, the homeward-bound Kentucky veterans of 1919 could not peer very far into the future. Felix Holt expressed a general sentiment by writing that "it will not be long until we are on our way. And it can't be too soon for me." Readjusting to civilian life held out no fears for Holt. Amusing himself and his family with a few lines of verse, he expressed the overwhelming readiness of Pershing's doughboys to bid the army goodbye:

> *To my Cap. I leave my cooties,*
> *To the Loot I leave the fleas,*
> *To my Top Soak I leave my bawl outs,*
> *The ones he gave to me.*
>
> *　＊　＊　＊*
>
> *To the Frogs I leave vin blanc and rouge,*
> *The francs and centimes too,*
> *But to my Pal I leave these words,*
> *"Let good luck be with you."*

3

REMEMBER PEARL HARBOR!

HUSBAND E. KIMMEL never lost his bitterness over 7 December 1941. "What's kept me alive," maintained the admiral from Henderson, Kentucky, "is to expose the entire Pearl Harbor affair." On a balmy Sunday morning, Admiral Nagumo's Japanese aircraft-carrier strike force had caught the United States Pacific Fleet lolling in port. The deadly surprise attack cost the United States nearly a score of sunk or damaged ships, numerous aircraft destroyed on the ground, and almost three thousand lives. As "CincPac" Kimmel commanded the fleet, holding the most coveted operational command in the American navy. Within hours after the Japanese onslaught, he and his army counterpart, Lt. Gen. Walter C. Short, had relinquished their commands. Not until 1945 were they assured that they would not be court-martialed.

Realistically, Kimmel should not have been surprised that his superiors saddled him with blame for a debacle that destroyed for months to come the offensive power of the American fleet. The military services have traditionally dealt harshly with command failures. Kimmel and Short were certainly at fault for neglecting to coordinate their respective commands, for omitting to disperse their ships and planes, and for failing to detect with air patrols and a primitive radar system the approach of the Japanese bombers. Moreover, Admiral Kimmel was very much a leader of the navy's so-called Gun Club, the dominant faction within the officer corps. These battleship admirals had not fully comprehended the ongoing transformation being forced upon naval strategy by the submarine, the amphibious force, and the aircraft carrier. The destruction of battleship row at Pearl Harbor wrote a symbolic finis to an era of naval history that went back to England's defeat of the Spanish Armada in 1588.

But Kimmel never reconciled himself to his role as the chosen scapegoat for mistakes and oversights that reached the highest levels of the presidential administration of Franklin D. Roosevelt. Although it did not become public knowledge until after 1945, American cryptologists had cracked Japan's diplomatic code more than a year before Pearl Harbor. The masses of raw data from intercepted diplomatic dispatches did not conclusively point to an attack on Hawaii but did indicate to top-level officials in the State, War, and Navy departments that a Japanese attack somewhere in the Pacific was imminent. Kimmel and Short knew nothing of the "Magic" decoder, however, and aside from a vaguely worded "war warning" broadcast to all field commanders on November 27 they received no advance warning from Washington. Most historians have attributed the failure to disseminate the potentially priceless intelligence to an understandable desire to keep from the Japanese the secret of the cryptological breakthrough. But Kimmel and a handful of postwar revisionist writers steadfastly contended that the Roosevelt administration had callously withheld vital information from him in the expectation that a Japanese attack would shock the enormously powerful, but still neutral, American goliath into fighting the Axis powers. The American people still clung to peace some four years after the Japanese had invaded China and two years after Germany had overwhelmed Poland. At the time of Pearl Harbor, Japan was reaching toward southeastern Asia and the Dutch East Indies, and Germany held Europe from the Atlantic Ocean to the outskirts of Moscow.

Most Americans were stunned by the news of Pearl Harbor; always they would remember the moment they heard it. The nation had started a partial mobilization for hemispheric defense in 1939, and in 1941 began sending "all aid short of war" to Great Britain, Nationalist China, and the Soviet Union. Nevertheless, it was sobering to realize that America was no longer only a ringside spectator of the Second World War.

At the University of Kentucky students listened to the radio, "in most cases calmly." So that all might hear President Roosevelt's war message to Congress on December 8, classes were dismissed. The *Kentucky Kernel* reported that "many students wore long faces and some of the girls broke into tears." Yet there were indications that initial alarm and outrage were soon tempered by relief that the prolonged, suspense-filled period of neutrality was over at last. "Now I can stop worrying about when we're going to war," declared one graduate student, "because now we're in it." A freshman coed agreed that the war "was something that had to come and it was lucky that we got into it this way." A male sophomore exclaimed, "Thank goodness I've got a bad leg and can't go. Hope we beat hell out of those squinty-eyed things!" The conflict was likely to be protracted, Professor Jasper Shannon warned bleakly. It might well last two years! The university's President Herman L. Donovan underscored Shannon's view of the need to take a long-term, measured approach to the hard days ahead, declaring that at the moment "the best service a student . . . can give . . . is to continue [his academic] preparation" and await his country's call.

In the faraway Philippines some sixty-six Kentuckians from Mercer County were already endangered by a Japanese tide poised to roll across the weakly held islands. Moreover, the Americans would defend themselves with resources already at hand, the Pearl Harbor disaster having wiped out any realistic hope of support by the beleaguered Pacific Fleet. The Kentuckians had entered federal service a year earlier, with the call-up of the active reserves. Most Kentucky National Guardsmen had reported to Camp Shelby, Mississippi, but the men from Harrodsburg, an understrength light-tank company, went to Fort Knox, where they became Company D of the 192d Tank Battalion. Ordered overseas in the fall of 1941, the tankers landed in Manila on Thanksgiving Day. In charge of the company during its long and fateful ocean voyage was Harrodsburg's Lt. Edwin W. Rue, who had joined the National Guard back in 1934 for fellowship and a few extra dollars.

In the Philippines all tank units were grouped in a provisional command under Brig. Gen. James R. N. Weaver, who assigned Lieutenant Rue as his liaison officer at the Fort Stotsenburg headquarters of Maj. Gen. Jonathan M. Wainwright's North Luzon Force. In overall command in the islands, Gen. Douglas MacArthur was to take the tankers under his direct control once the war began. As a liaison officer Rue was to have a remarkable vantage point in the most heart-rending defeat of America's military history. Well before December 8 (the seventh in Hawaii), there were clear indications that war might break out at any moment. Sightings of Japanese planes and troopships were reported, and American soldiers received orders to wear wartime clothing until further notice. Rue remembers hearing unconfirmed reports of Pearl Harbor at Fort Stotsenburg on the morning of the eighth. (Hours earlier, MacArthur and his staff had received official word of the attack.) General Weaver decided to send Rue over to Clark Field, where it would be the tankers' mission to repel any attack by Japanese paratroopers. As Rue's driver deposited him at the airfield's headquarters, the man pointed into the distance, saying matter-of-factly, "Look at that flight of planes." It was lunchtime, and the headquarters adjutant asked Rue to answer the telephone during his absence. Hardly had the adjutant departed before two waves of Japanese bombers—the distant specks spotted minutes earlier by Rue's driver—roared over the field. There was no advance warning at Clark Field of the attack. Somehow, neither MacArthur's staff nor that of Maj. Gen. Lewis H. Brereton, commanding the United States Far East Air Force, had authorized any precautionary measures at the base. (Unlike Admiral Kimmel, both MacArthur and Brereton remained in active service and rose to higher rank.) Alone in the second story of headquarters, Rue stood atop a safe to peer out of a high window and watch as Japanese fighters followed the bombers and methodically strafed the neatly parked rows of Flying Fortress bombers and P-40 fighters, thus eliminating with one lethal thrust the air support upon which prewar plans for defending the Philippines had largely rested. Amid the raging inferno of destruction, the headquarters building remained an island of safety. Rue donned a gas mask to protect himself from smoke inhalation.

He spent the next couple of weeks at general headquarters in

Manila's walled city, where he daily saw MacArthur at first hand during the lowest point of the general's remarkable up-and-down career. Nearly four decades after experiencing defeat and captivity in a campaign in which MacArthur was clearly not at his best, Rue generously remembers the general as "one of the greatest military minds that ever lived."

Two weeks after their initial air attacks, the Japanese splashed ashore at Lingayen Gulf, a hundred miles north of Manila. Over the coming weeks Edwin Rue was in constant motion between the tankers and various higher headquarters. Danger, exhaustion, and sheer nervous exhilaration made this the "most exciting" period of his life. He never forgot the "blood-red sunset" and "rippled clouds" of Christmas 1941.

On December 24 MacArthur evacuated Manila, concentrating his American and Filipino troops on Bataan Peninsula, between Manila Bay and the South China Sea. MacArthur established his headquarters on Corregidor Island, The Rock, just south of Bataan. During the move to Bataan and throughout the defense of the peninsula, the American tanks acted as a sort of fire brigade in support of the infantry. A member of the Harrodsburg company, John E. Sadler recounted his experiences in 1961: "We started running . . . first to one hole, to another one, or to places they thought the Japs were creeping through. And doing the best we could. There weren't too many places you could take those tanks. If you get off the road, you was gone. They'd sink in clear up above the tracks." As the Filipino-American army steadily lost ground, the tanks slowed the enemy advance with numerous small-scale counterattacks. On Russian steppes or African deserts the thin-skinned, lightly armed tanks of Bataan would have been worthless, but in the peninsula's dense jungles they proved their value. After the surrender the Japanese professed disbelief that the Americans had begun the campaign with only 108 tanks.

Back at Fort Knox Edwin Rue had wondered whether the Kentucky National Guardsmen were absorbing their training, but now they fought well. Only once anywhere on Bataan did he personally observe an American case of "buck fever"—an officer who sat laughing nervously and "couldn't go." Unfortunately, except for the regular-army Philippine Division, the Filipinos on Bataan were too poorly trained to make good soldiers. According to John Sadler the Americans sometimes "put the Filipino army up in front of us with the Americans behind them with machine guns, and if they turned and come back, the Americans would kill them. And if they stayed, the Japs would kill them. And they held those lines 'til it smelled so bad that you'd have to put on a gas mask to stand the scent."

The Americans had begun the defense of Bataan with plenty of ammunition, but with a critical shortage of replacement parts for vehicles and weapons. They eventually ran out of medicine, but even earlier many men had resisted taking the bitter-tasting quinine that might have shielded them from the deadly malaria-bearing mosquitoes infesting the peninsula. Along with countless others Edwin Rue contracted beriberi, to which he was vulnerable from malnutrition. No meat except for "bones with a little reddish tint to them" reached the front lines through a deadly gauntlet of strafing Japanese planes. As best they could, men subsisted off the country. "We eat anything from monkeys on down [to] small birds," said John Sadler. Edwin Rue adds that when the opportunity arose wandering carabao were slaughtered and eaten, a practice halted by rumors that the Japanese were prodding these water buffalo toward the American lines after dosing them with poison. Correct or not, the rumors were characteristic of the marvelous proficiency of the Japanese at psychological warfare. They stealthily infiltrated the American and Filipino positions, making their attacks in rainstorms or under the cover of darkness, a time when their screams were especially effective at rattling the nerves of the defenders. So well did the invaders conceal themselves that Edwin Rue never actually saw a Japanese soldier, although he believes himself to have been often "in their line of fire."

By March it was clear that Bataan was doomed, and MacArthur, his family and staff left for Australia in compliance with a directive from President Roosevelt. The majority of MacArthur's soldiers apparently retained confidence in his military skill, and Rue was glad to see the general get away, since someone who "knew the situation" appeared to be the most likely person to bring help to the Philippines. The Kentuckian recalls the tragic

General Wainwright, who had inherited MacArthur's Philippine command, as being "not only an officer, but a soldier."

At the outset of the campaign, the American high command had quickly grasped the impossibility of receiving substantial help. But the lower echelons live on fantastic rumors such as one making the rounds in December 1941 to the effect that crated planes were being hastily unloaded and assembled on the docks of Manila, and then were taking off down Dewey Boulevard. By the beginning of April defeat was an imminent certainty, and the morale of the defenders plummeted. From concealed advance listening posts had come reports of truckload upon truckload of fresh Japanese troops rolling toward the front. Their final offensive began on April 3, and six days later seventy-six thousand men, including some twelve thousand Americans, laid down their arms. More than three harrowing years were to pass before any of the Kentucky tankers saw the Bluegrass State again.

The defenders of Bataan had performed the traditional mission of the regular army; they had held their ground while an aroused America armed itself to take the offensive. Their sacrifice had bought dearly almost five months of precious time. No other American combatants in World War II would have to fight under such hopeless conditions.

In the United States hundreds of thousands of new recruits and draftees swelled the armed forces. From a mid-year strength of 458,365 in 1940, the ranks burgeoned to 1.8 million in 1941, and 3.85 million in 1942, peaking in 1945 at 12.1 million. The total to serve throughout the war was 16.1 million, including 305,272 from Kentucky. The Bluegrass State furnished 1.8 percent of the national military manpower of World War II. Kentucky's 6,211 battle deaths were 2.1 percent of the national total of 291,557.

Even more than in World War I the United States tried through selective service to allocate its manpower rationally and effectively. Deferments and exemptions were granted to meet national economic and social needs, and there was an attempt to train those who did enter the services in the military occupational specialties for which they were best suited. But events steadily altered the services' allocations of manpower. The army's pre-Pearl

Harbor Victory Program had forecast a peak wartime army mobilization of 8.8 million, only six hundred thousand more than the total eventually raised. But the program's projected 213 army combat divisions were more than twice the 91 actually formed. The United State Marine Corps was to deploy another 6 divisions. By way of comparison, the Soviet Union fielded over four hundred divisions, Germany three hundred, and Japan a hundred. The American planners had failed to anticipate an enormous need for infantry individual replacements, a mushrooming of the army's air forces, or the immense logistical tail required to sustain in ground combat a comparatively small fighting head. By 1944 Allied planners were calculating at a lavish seven hundred tons the daily requirement of supplies for a vehicle-heavy American division. A German division could fight very effectively with two hundred tons, but admittedly without the operational mobility of an American division. The burdens of ground fighting were not equitably distributed. A triangular (three infantry regiments) American division of 1944 contained about 14,000 men, with the 3,240 assigned to its eighty-one rifle platoons suffering 83 percent of its battle losses. Only one of every sixteen American soldiers in the European Theater of Operations in 1944–45 served in rifle platoons, although of course many others fought as machine gunners, tankers, artillerymen, or engineers.

Once men went on active duty they were entirely under federal control until their release. The War Department was frankly unsympathetic to state and regional loyalties (unlike the British and German armies) and freely shuffled its men like interchangeable parts from unit to unit. Moreover, the army organizations of 1940–42 were repeatedly "cannabilized" to form the cadres of new outfits, which then could be fleshed out with new inductees. By the time the 38th Division fought in 1945 to liberate the Philippines, many of the Kentuckians who had gone with the division to Camp Shelby were serving in other units. Still, to the end of the war the National Guard organizations retained a hard core of their original men, and even in 1945 the 149th Infantry Regiment and 138th Field Artillery Battalion of the 38th Division were the most distinctly Kentuckian units in the army.

Many thousands of volunteers came forward between 1940 and

1945. Their motivation was a sincere desire to serve—or the realization that they would otherwise be drafted. But few men wanted to be doughboys. The danger, discomfort, and absence of glamour of the infantry made it the most dreaded army branch of service. Overall, the public image of the various ground branches was less favorable than those of the naval and air services. And for the comparative handful of men who actually relished the prospective challenge of front-line combat, an attractive alternative to the infantry was offered by the Marine Corps, a brigade of which had made a spectacular reputation on the Western Front in 1918. William E. Barber of West Liberty, Kentucky, enlisted in the marines early in 1940 because he was attracted to the military and anxious to serve with "the best." The "most impressive veterans" Barber had encountered were former marines.

Much more typical were those Kentuckians who gravitated into a variety of essential combat-support assignments and officer-candidate programs. John D. Minton, a University of Kentucky senior from Trigg County, managed to get himself admitted to a navy midshipmen's course at Northwestern University. Harry L. Jackson, a National Guardsman from Bowling Green with experience in art and journalism, eventually wound up as a regimental public-information officier in the 30th Division. Weldon P. Shouse, a Lexington lawyer, won a commission in the Military Police Corps, despite a childhood history of osteomyelitis.

Unless men entered the army with reserve or direct commissions, they passed first through basic combat indoctrination, no matter what their subsequent assignments were to be. Harry Caudill, a University of Kentucky prelaw student from Whitesburg, decided in retrospect that his rugged weeks of basic training at Camp Croft, South Carolina, had not been "hard enough" to prepare him adequately for the ordeal of battle in Italy. For Lowell H. Harrison of Bowling Green, basic training at Fort Knox was especially memorable because of strenuous eight-mile road marches that always ended with a double-time sprint up "Agony Hill." Reflecting the recent fighting in North Africa, training at Fort Knox placed heavy emphasis upon "water discipline." Recruits had to make do on a single canteen of water per day for washing, shaving, brushing teeth—and drinking. But no trainee went hungry. From Fort Hayes, Ohio, D. Carl Perguson, Jr., described army-style dining: "After lining up in a column of twos, we walk to the door of the mess hall, which is so large that about 500 can be fed at one time. From the door we walk rapidly, almost running, around the hall passing several huge food containers where a big spoon-ful of each kind of food is slapped on the big metal tray, which is divided into sections. One of the boys noted the time yesterday, and only eight minutes passed from the time we entered the hall until we walked out with stomachs comfortably filled."

Assignment to "good duty" was no guarantee against a future change of orders. As a member of the Army Specialized Training Program, Lowell Harrison was placed in the preengineering curriculum at New York University. His company area (where men were free to go without passes) covered about half of Greenwich Village. And Harry Caudill was slated to go to the University of Michigan to prepare for service in the postwar occupation of Germany as a second lieutenant. But mounting battlefield losses by the end of 1943 convinced the army to curtail or abolish such programs as an unacceptable waste of manpower. Most of the men were reassigned as combat troops. Caudill read the bad news in a Sunday paper in November 1943. He recalls that "chagrin was the order of the day" among the men of his provisional outfit.

On 8 November 1942 American and British troops invaded Morocco and Algeria in North Africa. The Allies were in no way ready to open a true Second Front in northwestern Europe, but President Roosevelt had insisted that before the end of 1942 American ground forces be sent into action against the Germans, the strongest of the Axis partners. The landings of the Western Task Force in Morocco were staged directly from Norfolk, Virginia. The assignment of supervising the combat-loading of two ships in the invasion convoy had fallen to William R. Buster, a career artillery officer from Harrodsburg, Kentucky.

Although the Western Task Force made its way safely to North Africa, it was to be mid-1943 before the Allied navies definitely held the upper hand in the North Atlantic. Alone among World War II battles, that of the Atlantic lasted from September 1939 to the surrender of Germany. It is chilling to contemplate the probable outcome of the war had Nazi submarines succeeded in cutting Britain's maritime lifelines. Despite remarkable British successes in deciphering the radio codes by which the German naval high command directed its U-boats, the Germans sank 2,603 Allied merchant ships totaling 13.5 million tons.

A participant in the Battle of the Atlantic from the beginning of the war until after D Day was Commodore William J. Marshall, the onetime gunboat officer on the Yangtze. In command of the U.S.S. *Winslow*, Marshall received credit for sinking a U-boat off the mouth of the Amazon. The silhouette of the American destroyer resembled a certain class of cruisers, and in firing torpedoes at her bow and stern the German skipper fortunately miscalculated his target's length, and thus her range. Both torpedoes missed. The *Winslow* raced back up the track of the torpedoes, firing depth charges. Although oil and debris eventually bubbled to the surface, Marshall always believed that they were actually a successful ruse to permit the U-boat to escape.

By 1943 Marshall had assumed command of a squadron of half a dozen so-called tin cans that escorted merchantmen to the Anglo-American "chop line" in the mid-Atlantic. Zigzagging constantly, convoys were nevertheless held to the speed of their slowest ships. Marshall especially remembers one Russia-bound convoy from which he lost one ship before releasing his charges to the Royal Navy north of Iceland. From the meeting point to Murmansk, he later learned, German U-boats and aircraft from Norway wreaked havoc. Many of the precious lend-lease supplies intended for the Soviet Union disappeared without a trace beneath the icy Arctic seas.

If the Germans failed to prevent the passage across the Atlantic of American ground forces, the soldiers did sometimes find the voyage to be unnerving. The Western Task Force vessel aboard which Sgt. Chester Mercer, a native of Albany, Kentucky, sailed for Africa had to put back into Norfolk. The passengers and cargo were transferred to a liberty ship which then ran at full speed with an escort of two destroyers to overtake the invasion armada. Somewhat later in the war Lowell Harrison found shipboard conditions so crowded that exercising, washing, and eating all had to be done in shifts. However, seasickness steadily shrank the once-long chow lines. And at the beginning of 1944 Harry Caudill and the entire 85th Division were crammed into a single ocean liner, the onetime *Empress of Japan*, for a high-speed, unescorted run from New Jersey to Africa. Caudill's particular company was "scrotched for room" in the "bottom-most" hold, far below the waterline. The men slept in suspended hammocks filling virtually all of the space in the hold. At night one could "measure by the curses" the progress of individuals climbing downward from hammock to hammock to visit the "head."

The British were eager to get on with a series of Mediterranean campaigns because of their traditional interest in that region. But Gen. George C. Marshall, chief-of-staff of the American army, regarded the entire theater as an expensive sideshow delaying the main event: a cross-channel invasion of northern France. The Germans in Africa surrendered in May 1943, which was too late to permit the opening of the Second Front that year. Because it was unthinkable for the large Anglo-American forces in the Mediterranean to await idly the great endeavor of the war, they invaded Sicily in July 1943 and in September moved into southern Italy. The agonizingly slow advance up the Italian boot lasted for the rest of the war. If the Mediterranean was a secondary theater, it nevertheless brought certain advantages to the Allies. Contained in Africa and southern Europe were German troops who might have been sent to other fronts. The opening of the Mediterranean permitted shipments of war matériel to Russia by way of the Suez Canal and Iran. And from African and Italian bases British and American bombers pounded southern Germany and the Balkans.

Most importantly, the early fighting developed an effective team of experienced American divisions and field commanders under the overall direction of Gen. Dwight D. Eisenhower. The flamboyant Lt. Gen. George S. Patton, Jr., was undoubtedly the most dynamic American combat leader to emerge in North Africa and Sicily. Patton reinvigorated the lackluster II Corps in Tunisia in March and April of 1943, then led the Seventh Army through the Sicilian campaign. Patton projected his high-strung personality to his troops, whereas most senior commanders remained shadowy figures to the men in the ranks. Among the first to learn that Patton had slapped the faces of hospitalized enlisted soldiers in Sicily was Walter W. Hillenmeyer, Jr., from Lexington, Kentucky, an aide to Maj. Gen. Clarence R. Huebner in command of the 1st Division. Huebner refused to believe the slapping story when Hillenmeyer reported it, but it was soon confirmed by Lt. Gen. Omar N. Bradley, head of the II Corps in Patton's Seventh Army. Patton's harshness and bombast were balanced by a personal magnetism that usually won the loyalty of subordinate commanders and staff officers. Often coarse of speech, Patton was also devout, traits that the general sometimes intermixed. At the cathedral in Palermo, Sicily, on 26 July 1943 Hillenmeyer and General Huebner watched at a distance while Patton paid a courtesy call upon the Roman Catholic cardinal. According to Patton's diary, "We went into a chapel and prayed." Hillenmeyer adds that Patton remained on his knees for some moments after the cardinal was ready to move on. Finally, Patton rose and led the way out of the chapel, asking under his breath as he passed Huebner, "Did you see how I outprayed that son of a bitch?"

From September 1943 until the invasion of Normandy nine months later, Italy was the largest active American ground theater. That even the comparatively small-scale fighting there was too huge to comprehend in its entirety at first hand is shown by the varied impressions it made upon three Kentucky participants, each of whom had a different vantage point. Laban P. Jackson, a reservist from Shelbyville, served throughout the campaign at headquarters of the American Fifth Army. As a lieutenant colonel, Jackson eventually headed the thousand or so "special troops" needed to keep in operation the nerve center of a fighting force of several hundred thousand soldiers of different nationalities. Army headquarters was a small town in its own right. Behind the combat zone, Captain Weldon Shouse was assigned to the Fifty Army's G-5 (military government) section, which supervised millions of Italian civilians, and attempted to keep civil unrest from draining manpower away from the Fifth and British Eighth armies. And up front Harry Caudill lived the nasty, brutish, and short life of an infantry rifleman: struggling to stay alive, to put food in his belly, and to find a warm, dry place to sleep.

Early on 9 September 1943 the Fifth stormed the beaches of

Salerno. Leading ashore a special advance party from army headquarters, Laban Jackson commandeered a jeep and located a suitable site for the command post of Lt. Gen. Mark W. Clark, the commanding general. By dark Jackson had found a castle, posted guards from a chemical battalion, and arranged maps in the war room. However, the Germans soon mounted a savage counterattack against the Allied landing, hastening to Salerno fresh troops from all over Italy. The Fifth Army battled desperately to cling to its precious toehold. About eleven o'clock on the first night ashore Maj. Gen. Alfred M. Gruenther, Clark's chief-of-staff, urgently told Jackson to relocate headquarters closer to the landing beaches, and to be sure that the heavy field safe containing the Fifth Army's secret documents did not fall into German hands. Jackson found for headquarters an olive grove two miles to the rear, and he deposited the precious safe with a graves-registration unit, assuming logically that the day's dead would be gathered at the safest point in the beachhead. Nearby was a tobacco factory where the United States VI Corps had set up its command post. The corps was in chaos, with the commanding general, as Jackson observed, speaking anxiously by field telephone directly to lower-echelon units, thus bypassing his divisional commanders.

Only the arrival ashore of a regiment of the veteran 45th Division "saved our skins," Jackson felt. The reinforcement steadied the green and badly mangled 36th. Jackson never abandoned his confidence that the Fifth Army would consolidate its lodgment, the alternative of an evacuation under enemy fire being too dismal to contemplate. As a precaution Gruenther did order the army's staff to work up a contingency plan for reembarkation. At the very moment that American soldiers stood face-to-face with catastrophe in Italy, Jackson remembers, he learned of a United Mine Workers' strike back in the United States. Jackson was outraged by the thought that the union's leaders felt no compunctions over striking in the midst of the war. The crisis at Salerno finally eased when the cautious advance of the British Eighth Army up the toe of the Italian boot compelled the Germans to break off the battle and withdraw to a new defensive line north of Naples.

One of a military-government contingent of several hundred, Weldon Shouse landed at Naples on the heels of the combat troops who had passed through after Salerno. The city was to be the logistical base for many dreary months of fighting yet to come, but it was also a severe administrative headache for the Allied high command. When the Germans evacuated Naples, remembers Shouse, "there was not a pigeon, there was not a cat—everything had been eaten." It came as no surprise to him that a staggering proportion of the Allied rations and military supplies crossing the docks of the city wound up in the hands of the Neapolitan black market.

North of Naples Shouse worked with a small military-government team administering a series of rural towns for periods of two or three months. In each community the Americans restored water, electricity, postal deliveries, fire and police protection, courts, and municipal government. Shouse once dismissed a mayor upon discovering that the man was the local secretary of the Fascist party. To his chagrin he learned a week later that his own appointee was the Fascist chief. Despite such problems Shouse came to like and to form warm friendships with Italians.

More than a score of Kentuckians eventually served with G-5 in Italy. Back in Africa, where Shouse had helped to organize an Anglo-American military-government team in anticipation of the early fall of Rome, he made no secret of his preference for men from his own state. The G-5 staff section was headed, incidentally, by General Erskine Hume of Frankfort. Military government was unquestionably good duty. By his own admission Weldon Shouse lived during the last year of the war a life that would have been the envy of a millionaire in the United States. Shouse's immediate superior, Col. Robert P. Marshall, exhorted his officers to sequester "suitable quarters," by which he meant "the best there was." Especially in central and northern Italy the best quarters were palatial. "I was not uncomfortable," Shouse fondly recalls.

From late 1943 to the following May the struggle for Italy was stalemated, the Germans at the mountaintop monastery of Monte Cassino blocking the Allied route to Rome. Preparations for the Normandy invasion voraciously consumed Anglo-American resources that might have broken the deadlock. Largely to quiet the incessant verbal proddings of Prime Minister Winston Churchill, who took a proprietary interest in the British-commanded Mediterranean theater, the Fifth Army mounted a "cat-claw" amphibious landing at the west-coast beach resort of Anzio on 22 January 1944. The Allies hoped to trap the defenders of Cassino, while simultaneously opening the southern door to the Eternal City.

Laban Jackson shepherded to Anzio the top ground commander in Italy, Sir Harold Alexander, along with General Clark and assorted lesser lights. On a dark night Jackson brought his party of brass hats to the Volturno River, down which they were to travel by powered skiffs to a rendezvous with PT boats at its mouth. To Jackson's dismay the river fog was so heavy that he could scarcely make out his own hand, let alone find the skiffs. To his relief the faint outline of a familiar bombed-out bridge appeared through the mist to give him his bearings.

At Anzio the VI Corps landed without opposition. Locating a jeep, Jackson drove inland some fifteen miles without sighting a single German. He was convinced that the road to Rome was wide open, but the painfully cautious Maj. Gen. John P. Lucas, the landing-force commander, laboriously built up a secure bridgehead instead of thrusting toward Rome. Perhaps Lucas was right to fear that a premature advance would meet with disaster, but his deliberate approach gave the Germans priceless time to rush divisions from distant points to contain and counterattack the Allied lodgment. Within days the original attackers were themselves the besieged. No place in their defensive perimeter was beyond the range of Anzio Annie, a massive German railroad gun, shells from which gave off a sound "like an express train." The unceasing January and February rains turned much of the terrain around Anzio into an impassable quagmire. British and American spirits lifted only after General Lucas gave way to Maj. Gen. Lucian K. Truscott, Jr., whom Jackson came to know well. A two-fisted drinker, the taciturn Truscott was "not a showman, but he did inspire confidence."

Jackson returned to Fifth Army headquarters in time to witness on 15 February 1944 perhaps the most controversial destructive act of the war: the aerial bombardment of the historic abbey atop Monte Cassino. Especially vivid in his memory is the sight of one plane releasing its bombs short of the monastery, thus hitting an American gun emplacement near where Jackson was watching.

Laying waste to the abbey was, of course, one of many Allied efforts to penetrate the seemingly impregnable German defensive line, of which Monte Cassino was the keystone. All attempts to break through during the late-winter months of 1944 were to fail. Acknowledging the magnitude of his task, General Alexander carefully laid the groundwork for an elaborate one-two punch offensive by the Fifth and Eighth armies and by the VI Corps in Anzio. He would attack in May, when the weather would be better.

Arriving in Italy in anticipation of the great forward surge was Harry Caudill of the 85th Division, which around April Fools' Day replaced in the front line a British Division that for weeks had contested with the Germans the possession of a certain ridge. Hundreds of British and American graves dotted the hill in mute testimony of the intensity and inconclusiveness of the recent fighting. A youthful and optimistic twenty-one, Caudill expected to survive the war, but he was nonetheless disturbed by the burial site of a Private Ronald Cole, a British Coldstream Guardsman who had been about Harry's own age. It was unsettling to wonder what sort of person Cole had been and to speculate about the unfulfilled promise of his life. Caudill was also bothered by the sight of an unburied German corpse. In contrast, the Germans across the way apparently took scrupulous care of Allied bodies.

For weeks the front was quiet except for constant patrols by both sides in the No Man's Land between the lines. For green soldiers these nighttime probes were an overwhelming experience. All sounds were exaggerated in the darkness, which heightened both uncertainty and anxiety.

The 85th Division soon received visits from the high command. Caudill helped dig a trench deep enough for the generals to walk upright and under cover to a forward observation post. General Clark and theater-commander Sir Henry Maitland "Jumbo" Wilson were tall men, so the trench had to be deep. Wisely, only one top-level officer went forward at any one time. According to Caudill, the men of the 85th Division believed Alexander, Clark, and their subordinate commanders to be capable professionals who did "a remarkably good job" of managing a difficult campaign over forbidding terrain and with only a low-priority claim on Allied resources.

Even in April Caudill and his comrades were exposed to the peninsula's cold, sleety rains. Everywhere there were stones that cut through the shoes and trousers of the American GIs. In May Caudill had a strange encounter near the front with an elderly Italian civilian. In idiomatic American English the man declared that for three decades he had worked in the United States for the Chesapeake and Ohio Railroad, and that he had retired back to Italy, only to be caught in the war. He urged Caudill to remember him to friends in the faraway Kentucky towns of Neon and Jenkins.

All along the main Allied line and at the Anzio beachhead preparations for the coming battle intensified. Many American divisions shifted to Anzio by sea, while the bulk of the British Eighth Army quietly replaced them on the western side of the Apennine Mountains, spinal cord of the Italian peninsula. On the extreme left of the main line, the 85th Division rested in anticipation of a May 12th assault. The climactic battle for Rome was timed to begin just under a month before the landings in northwestern Europe.

Late in the evening of May 11 the ground shuddered with the ear-splitting roar of an artillery barrage of the German positions. The throb of aircraft engines announced the arrival of tactical bombers. Enjoined to keep down, Harry Caudill and his friends could not deny themselves a spectacle equal to a hundred July 4th displays rolled into one. To the American infantrymen it was beyond belief that anyone could live through such a crescendo of destruction. Caudill's regiment, the 337th Infantry, was held back as the divisional reserve while the other two regiments jumped off. As they did so, Caudill could hear the high-pitched chatter of German machine guns. Despite a hail of German bullets, the 85th somehow made headway.

On the thirteenth Caudill's outfit leapfrogged the division's other two regiments to exploit their initial gains. Knowing that the call to move up would inevitably come, Caudill had found waiting on the fringe of battle an agony. It was a relief to go ahead. In a stream he saw floating American bodies; their heavy uniforms were filled with air "like balloons." The sound of German machine guns aroused Caudill's "outrage and indignation" that any of the enemy should have defied probability and survived the bombardment, and that they were contesting fiercely the progress of the American infantry. The artillery had demolished every building within range, but Italians "build for the ages," and the rubble of their devastated houses made splendid improvised fortresses. Yet the guns had definitely softened up the defenses. German prisoners were usually temporarily deaf, and from their ears and noses oozed blood.

Day after day the 85th Division made slow gains up the coast road. Supply trucks and pack mules brought mostly ammunition and medicine to the front lines, leaving Caudill and his fellow soldiers with empty stomachs. Under the circumstances a third of a can of cheese seemed like a rare delicacy. Hunger and exhaustion numbed the pain of losing one's friends. After a few days of combat and with no opportunity for daily ablutions, Caudill's mouth came to feel as if it were filled with "a great growth of fuzz."

On May 18 he learned from the lieutenant of his platoon that he would have to take over as its sergeant. Death, wounds, and straggling (attributable more to exhaustion than malingering) had in only six terrible and confusing days decimated the original ranks. As the lieutenant pointed out, it was the "old men" who now would have to reconstitute the outfit.

Caudill never got to wear his stripes as platoon sergeant. With his advancing company he was pinned down by German machine guns and mortars just two hours after the conversation with the lieutenant. Told to stand fast in its exposed position, the company anxiously awaited help that did not come. Caudill tried to get help from the American main line some thirty-five yards to the rear. As he crawled back he could hear overhead the shells of German artillery. Infantrymen in battle quickly develop "a feeling" about incoming fire—whether it is high, low, or on target. Usually, however, it is impossible for a foot soldier to know if the distant, unseen cannoneers are merely firing patterns, or if he himself has been seen and bracketed by an artillery spotter. Sighted or not, Caudill received in his leg a shell fragment that struck like "a sledgehammer." Gushing blood from the wound filled his shoe. Finding temporary safety with his comrades in an irirgation ditch, Caudill managed to halt the bleeding with a tourniquet improvised from his own belt. Some time afterward, the company was withdrawn from the ditch, but it was not possible to evacuate a wounded man. A medical corpsman handed over two Syrettes of morphine, sternly warning that Caudill must not be misled by a drug-induced euphoria into neglecting the tourniquet. Unless he eased the pressure occasionally he would lose the leg. The next few hours the wounded Caudill spent alone in No Man's Land, but his company returned around one that morning. The Germans had broken off their skillful delaying action and withdrawn northward.

Four cursing litter-bearers painfully carried the wounded man back to the divisional aid station, where, with tweezers, a Captain Freeman removed the shell fragment. It resembled a piece of cast-iron stove. Only Caudill's anguished protests saved the leg from immediate amputation. The doctors decided instead to ship the patient to the general hospital at Naples, where to his relief the leg gradually began healing. Most of the original members of Caudill's infantry company also passed through the Naples hospital; only eight or nine finished the war still with the company. Its commander, called the Kindly Old Captain by his men, had been killed in the May 12th jump-off. Weeks later, Harry Caudill was evacuated to the United States. For him the war was over.

The great Allied offensive rolled laboriously northward. The VI Corps opened the second phase of Operation Diadem when it surged out of Anzio some eleven days after the first attacks from the main line. A day after the second breakout Weldon Shouse drove through Anzio. Laid out in nearby fields he saw the collected bodies of several thousand soldiers killed during the long siege. In his jeep Shouse carried serum to combat a rumored typhus epidemic in Rome.

By the evening of June 4 the Allied armies had lunged to the outskirts of Rome. The Italian capital had been declared an open city by Field Marshal Kesselring, the German commander, so the men of the Fifth Army had orders not to shoot if they could avoid doing so. On the lookout, as always, for a suitable location for Fifth Army headquarters, Laban Jackson entered Rome late on the fourth. A German machine gun at the Colosseum halted him temporarily, but it was gone the next morning. Jackson found his way to the bar at the Excelsior Hotel. Aside from a civilian of undisclosed nationality (who claimed to be a count) and his blonde companion, the place was deserted. At the Villa Borghese, the largest public park in the city, Jackson established the command post. That night his headquarters special troops flushed from the famous gardens no fewer than forty-five German stragglers.

Once it was certain that the Germans were gone, the Romans thronged the streets, celebrating with wild abandon the dramatic climax of the war in Italy. But within weeks seven veteran American and French-colonial divisions had been taken from Alexander and Clark to land in the South of France. The force left behind in Italy was not strong enough to break through the next major German position, the Gothic Line, until the spring of 1945. The post-Rome letdown was typical of the Italian theater, where, as Laban Jackson has said, the fighting was "all uphill" and both commanders and troops felt shortchanged of their "fair share" of Allied equipment and manpower.

After Rome the troops in the peninsula were largely ignored by the press and public—on 6 June 1944 British and American troops landed in Normandy, creating at last the long-anticipated Second Front.

Without question Operation Overlord was the riskiest and most complex Allied military enterprise of the war. Years of planning and preparation had preceded it. The great invasion might well have failed had the Germans not been misled about its exact date and place by various Allied deceptive measures. In England a fictitious army group under General Patton filled the air waves with bogus radio messages. So seriously did the Germans take the threat of a landing by Patton at the Pas de Calais that they kept their entire Fifteenth Army in strategic reserve. In Italy the Allied spring offensive held in place the German reserves of that theater. And all around the periphery of Europe British commandos and Americans from the Office of Strategic Services confused the enemy further with numerous raids and feints.

Based in Italy and commanding an OSS group of about two hundred men was Capt. Robert F. Houlihan of Lexington, Kentucky. Houlihan had studied classical Greek at a Jesuit secondary boarding school in Wisconsin. His language training made him a prize recruit for the OSS, the World War II forerunner of the Central Intelligence Agency. In addition to commando operations, the OSS gathered intelligence and engaged in clandestine espionage.

Houlihan's first raid had come in March 1944 against the German-held island of Solta, off the Dalmatian coast. (An advance group of "beach jumpers" under the movie actor Lt. Cdr. Douglas Fairbanks, Jr., saw the raiding party of several hundred ashore from their landing craft.) About half of Houlihan's unit of Greek-Americans took part in this surprise attack, which wiped out most of the Germans garrisoning the town of Grohote.

Shortly afterward, Houlihan and three of his sergeants were sent to investigate the possibility of putting some OSS units into Yugoslavia. In a nondescript fishing boat they left the offshore island of Hvar and traveled to a mainland rendezvous with local Communist partisans. At a remote, mountaintop partisan headquarters, Houlihan noticed a certain woman. Her face, he remembers, was utterly without expression. She wore a kerchief, a red blouse, and a polka-dot shirt. He soon learned that she had just been convicted by a partisan "people's court" for collaborating with the Germans. At dark—the camp was completely blacked out to prevent detection by German planes—the woman was taken away. Soon the evening stillness was shattered by a single burst of Sten submachine-gun fire. When the firing squad returned a few moments afterward, most of the partisans gathered in a large captured Italian headquarters tent, where they began singing mournful Slavic dirges and sipping *rakija,* a local beverage described by Houlihan as a "Yugoslav moonshine" potent enough to ignite "a Zippo lighter."

By 1944 it appeared likely to the Allies that the Communists would prevail over the Yugoslav monarchists, so OSS personnel were instructed to cooperate with the Reds—not to argue politics. The partisan leaders impressed Houlihan as "top-drawer people," fiercely proud and nationalistic. In all, he spent about a month at the partisan stronghold—planning to depart on the next moonless night. Just before he left the leaders honored him with a feast of roast goat. Toasts were drunk to Tito, Churchill, Stalin, and Roosevelt. On the long downhill trek to their boat rendezvous, the Americans were pelted with flowers by excited villagers. The OSS men were easily recognizable since they wore regular military uniforms, a practice which Houlihan says "really helped us with the people." Reaching the pick-up cove at midnight, he and his sergeants were dismayed to find not their expected fishing craft but a German patrol boat escorting a barge. Hugging the ground, they distinctly heard German voices across the water, but they were not detected. Withdrawing from the dangerous shore, the Americans successfully arranged another rendezvous by radio.

Houlihan's mission produced no direct results; the Western Allies soon ended their brief flirtation with the Communist guerrillas of Yugoslavia. After Normandy Allied irregular warfare in the Mediterranean took place mainly in Greece and Italy, where considerable care was taken to keep military equipment away from Communists. Houlihan's unit received a presidential citation for its work in Greece—but Yugoslavia was discreetly left unmentioned at a time when the Cold War was already beginning. In retrospect, Houlihan is proud of his military service, but he confesses readily that he was "often frightened to death" behind the German lines. While there he vowed silently that "if I survive this . . . nothing will ever shake my equanimity." The far-flung twilight-warfare campaign in which Houlihan had participated had helped to assure victory on D Day.

More than deception was needed to make feasible the invasion of Normandy, however. During the first five months of 1944 the Anglo-American combined bomber offensive won the supremacy in the skies over Europe that provided the slender margin of victory in Normandy, where the Allied ground forces were comparatively small in relation to the magnitude of their task. Following stupendous losses of unescorted B-17 Flying Fortresses and B-24 Liberators, which had waged an ever-larger daylight-precision-bombing campaign in 1943, the Americans mounted range-extending special drop-tanks on their fighters, enabling them for the first time to escort the bombers to targets deep inside Germany. With mounting fury and accuracy, the bombers attacked the Germans' aircraft industry, substantially hindering production. The American raids forced the Luftwaffe into a hopeless battle of attrition in which German planes and fliers were steadily decimated by the American fighter escorts. Big Week in late February 1944 brought the triumphant climax of the struggle for air supremacy. Then, during the days and weeks just before the landing itself, the British and American air forces strafed and bombed French roads, bridges, and marshaling yards to seal off the ground battlefield from easy reinforcement. The crucial aerial battles of 1943–44 have been so vividly recounted in the memoir *Bomber Pilot*, by Philip Ardery, commander of a squadron of Liberators and a peacetime Kentucky lawyer, that there is no need here for a detailed description.

Shielded, then, by a "bodyguard of lies," and covered with an umbrella of airplanes, an immense Anglo-American invasion armada steamed toward the far shore of the English Channel. Fortune aided the Allies. The very storm that had postponed by twenty-four hours their amphibious assault had also convinced the Germans that no attack was imminent.

Minesweepers cleared the way to Omaha Beach, linchpin of the Normandy invasion. Escorting them were destroyers under Bill Marshall. From June 6 to the fall of Cherbourg three weeks later, Commodore Marshall directed from the U.S.S. *Tracy* some thirteen British and American tin cans, twenty-four United States PT boats, and twenty-four Royal Navy steam gunboats. The *Tracy* ran close enough to the beach to damage her starboard propeller. From the bridge Marshall watched American rangers scaling the hundred-foot cliff of Pointe du Hoe, using mortar-propelled grappling hooks and ropes. It was the rangers' mission to destroy an enemy battery of long-barreled guns with a range of twenty thousand yards and positioned to fire either at Omaha Beach or the British Gold Beach. The destroyers directed machine-gun fire at Germans who were sniping over the edge of the cliff at the oncoming rangers. Marshall's ships continued to respond to calls for fire from naval spotters on shore until the landings were consolidated several days later. From their close range the fast-moving vessels pinpointed enemy tanks and pillboxes, managing because of their speed and closeness to the shoreline to evade being hit by German artillery.

The honor, and ordeal, of storming Omaha Beach fell to the 1st Infantry Division under General Huebner, whose predecessor, the hell-for-leather Terry Allen, had led the Big One in Tunisia and Sicily. Allen's disdain for regulations had persuaded General Bradley, the senior American ground commander in Normandy, to place the experienced, but slack, division under the "flinty disciplinarian" Huebner. As the Old Man's aide, Walter Hillenmeyer had watched Huebner retrain the division. Dismayed to learn that only a quarter of his men were qualified marksmen, Huebner took strenuous measures to correct the deficiency. In January 1944 he placed his men on alert for the invasion, reminding them that any man who missed the boat would be court-martialed for desertion in the face of the enemy. One man was absent on D Day, although many had been delinquent in the Sicilian invasion. Huebner chose to retain most of the subordinate commanders and staff officers he had inherited from Allen, commenting to Hillenmeyer that at least with officers of known strengths and weaknesses he would be "playing poker with a marked deck."

Huebner and Hillenmeyer spent the early hours of 6 June 1944 in the message center of the U.S.S. *Ancon* while the assault waves of the Big Red One struggled across the bullet-swept Omaha Beach. The general had directed that all dispatches to the command ship be numbered consecutively. Message No. 4, the first to be received, painted a disheartening picture of the unfolding battle, but Huebner did not panic. When at last he could spread out No. 1 through No. 7, it was clear that—in spite of horrendous losses—the 1st Division was gradually fighting its way inland. By midafternoon Huebner had established his command post ashore.

In the hot stress of seven desperate weeks of battling across the thick hedgerows of Normandy, Anglo-American command disputes first rose to the surface. The excessively cautious Sir Bernard L. Montgomery, the senior Allied ground commander, was a capable tactician with a prickly manner that infuriated many of his American subordinates. Quarrels among allies are natural, and rivalries among ambitious (and egotistical) senior commanders are a part of every war. The failure of a British division to the left of the Big Red One to keep pace with the gains made by the Americans left Huebner's men with an exposed flank. The officers of the 1st Division, so Hillenmeyer remembers, respected the Tommies as dogged defensive fighters. When planning attacks, however, the British charted "great phase lines, but always forgot the first two hundred yards."

Hillenmeyer's duties as aide to the commander of a division in battle were scarcely those of a social secretary. He was constantly at Huebner's side, listening to and making notes of the Old Man's field-telephone conversations. In a dispersed organization of fourteen thousand men, a commander could control only those with whom he had communications. Thus, when Huebner visited subordinate commanders and forward troops, Hillenmeyer seized every opportunity to call headquarters to report the general's whereabouts and inquire about incoming messages. A self-contained organization with permanently assigned troops, a division was in Hillenmeyer's words "a family team." Although certainly not exposed to the risks run by a rifleman, a sleeping Hillenmeyer was nevertheless wounded in a Norman apple orchard when a shell burst in a nearby tree.

Among the divisions entering the beachhead shortly after D Day was the 30th, with which Capt. Harry L. Jackson served as an information officer. Even in the summertime, Jackson told his family, northern France had "foul" weather—cold nights and rain for "days on end." "I have been helping clear the battlefield of the dead, both American and German," he wrote in late June. "That is the most gruesome job I have ever undertaken. We dare not touch the bodies after we find them until we have tested them for Boobey Traps."

In late July the 30th Division was hard hit by American strategic bombers during the breakout from Normandy. Massive carpet bombing by fifteen hundred planes broke the stout German defenses, but "shorts" also inflicted some six hundred casualties upon the 30th and other American units. With the 2d Armored Division several miles back, Sgt. Chester Mercer watched the distant specks falling from the bombers. The very earth seemed to quiver under the impact of exploding bombs. Mercer doubted that any Germans could survive such destruction. Some did, of course, but not enough to contain the pent-up Allied flood. Infantry divisions, followed closely by two armored divisions, fought their way through the cratered terrain around Saint Lô, where the bombers had struck. The armor pushed its ways through the infantry and streamed into the open country beyond. A desperate yard-by-yard struggle had suddenly turned into mobile warfare.

At the point of the 2d Armored Division's spearhead were frequently teamed the fifty-two infantrymen of Chester Mercer's platoon with the five General Sherman mediums of a tank platoon. Mercer's GIs usually rode on the backs of their accompanying tanks. Meeting opposition, the point men would hold in place while reinforcements from the long column behind them deployed swiftly to encircle or bypass the Germans. Since tanks could fight effectively only in daylight, darkness nearly always brought armored advances to an overnight halt. On one unforgettable night, Mercer with an advance patrol heard from the rear the heavy rumble of armored vehicles. The lumbering shadows proved to be German tanks overrun by the swift American offensive. Mercer and his small party beat a hasty retreat, a wise precaution because the Germans sprayed their previous position with machine-gun fire.

The breakthrough was the first taste of battle for the 6th Armored Division, in which Lt. Col. Embry D. "Simon" Lagrew, a reservist from Lexington, Kentucky, headed the 15th Tank Battalion. Lagrew's outfit had seventy-seven tanks: three companies of Sherman mediums and a company of light tanks. In action Lagrew usually directed an improvised task force in which armored infantry, assault guns, combat engineers, antiaircraft artillery, and signalmen reinforced the tank battalion to form a versatile, powerful, and mobile team. Lagrew had devoted considerable advance thought to his own initiation into combat. (He describes himself as having been "chicken-hearted all my life," a characteristic of which he gave no outward evidence in action.) The mission of the 6th Armored was to drive southward on an axis parallel to that of the 2d and 3d armored divisions to its left, then swing westward into Brittany. Once it began to roll the American blitzkrieg of August 1944 swept ahead farther and faster than had the Germans during the 1940 conquest of France.

A demonic nervous energy somehow drove Lagrew and his men onward. Suffering a minor wound in Brittany, Lagrew shook off the pain with a shot of morphine from a medical corpsman and, later, some champagne from a French civilian. Over nine months of combat, Lagrew rarely got more than a few consecutive hours of sleep, yet he managed to function. From Brittany the 6th Armored shifted southward to L'Orient, where for some days it contained the garrison of that notorious German submarine base. Nearby, Lagrew's men captured thousands of cases of liquor. Simon held back fourteen truckloads for his own troops. Recognizing that men in combat did not "work union rules," and that they faced stern punishment if caught shooting prisoners of war (something of a problem during the early going), he accepted the necessity for leniency in some other matters. Many soldiers eagerly drank whatever spirits they could "liberate." During the pause at L'Orient Lagrew established a guarded area open to men whose units were temporarily out of the line. After handing over his weapons for safekeeping, a soldier could enter and drink his fill of the brandy and champagne from Lagrew's cache.

If it could be avoided, American Shermans never fought the more heavily armored and gunned German tanks without artillery support. The American armor tried instead to pierce the enemy's main line and disrupt his rear—leaving antitank guns to contend with the German Panthers and Tigers.

The American artillery was far superior to that of the Germans, and traced its tradition of excellence back to Henry Knox and Alexander Hamilton in the War of Independence. Having the Germans "outgunned" as they did, American cannoneers were "never really concerned" about German artillery, according to William Buster. Only five years out of West Point, Buster commanded the 2d Armored Division's 92d Armored Field Artillery Battalion. He directed 750 men and eighteen 105-millimeter self-propelled guns. In action Buster usually left his executive officer in charge of the battalion column, having discovered that "in an armored situation" it was better to be with the commander of the unit his gunners were supporting. Often, Buster could size up the other officer's fire-support needs without being told. Buster, his fire-controller, intelligence specialists, forward observers, and spotter pilots of Cubs flying at treetop level all became so proficient at reading terrain and evaluating the probable effect of meteorological conditions upon shell trajectory that they were able to radio precise map coordinates to the cannoneers with orders to "fire for effect." Without the advance warning given by the bracketing of targets, American shellfire was even more devastating.

Although serving in a combat arm, a field artilleryman lived a relatively tolerable life compared to that of an infantryman. The manpower roster of Buster's battalion remained fairly stable from Normandy to the heart of Germany. But when a shortage of infantrymen late in 1944 required sending some of his men to the 41st Armored Infantry Regiment, those who did not become casualties gained promotions for which they could not have hoped in the artillery, with its smaller losses. Buster observed that infantry soldiers who faced daily the agony of front-line combat tended to become withdrawn in personality, as if numbing themselves to the wretchedness of their lives. Harry Jackson with the 30th Division made much the same observation, commenting that "Sherman was only too right—'War *is* Hell!'" Its most trying aspect was not danger or discomfort: "Rather it's the look in men's eyes after they have come out of it—They are the living dead without fear, evil, or comfort." Jackson later wrote that he did not "believe there is anyone with imagination great enough to describe one's feeling in combat—It's not only fear—there is a certain thrill to it also . . . and a sickness in the pit of your stomach." Even during the breathtaking August 1944 race to the German border Jackson was struck by the fact that "the roads are strewn with the mangled wreckage of the implements of war, the dead, and the refugees." But he did succumb to the "mad and exciting" pleasure of being pelted with "flowers, fruit—kisses and most everything" by the newly liberated French people: "One old Frenchman . . . yelled at us 'Heep! Heep! Hurray!'"

Early in September Eisenhower's British and American armies ground to a halt. They had outrun their supply lines. For the next three months they would inch forward at a terrible cost through the rains and mud of the western frontier of Germany. Once again it was an infantryman's war; there were few openings for armor to exploit. Over many weeks Harry Jackson remained with the 30th Division near the Belgian-German border in a sector controlled by Lt. Gen. William H. Simpson's Ninth Army. In the 1944 presidential election it fell to Jackson to act as regimental voting officer: "It was such a farce to ask the men in the combat area to vote. Every time we mentioned voting to them they howled with derision. On many occasions it became necessary to crawl from foxhole to foxhole to deliver ballots and to take them up. Very few men voted." When winter set in Jackson and several others moved into "a small house . . . with a German family upstairs—the place is cold as fury." The lack of a working toilet was an annoyance: "The American male is a modest soul and does not like to have the entire populace staring him straight in the face upon such delicate occasions, but apparently it makes little difference to the average European, for when they feel the call they stop in the most unexpected places and let go with complete equanimity and aplomb regardless of who may be around."

In the First Army zone was the 104th Division, which had entered combat on October 23, a date remembered by Lowell Harrison because it was his birthday. As a combat engineer Harrison spent many nighttime hours in No Man's Land—either planting American mines or disarming German ones. About a fourth of the latter were booby-trapped, yet the need for haste often called for dangerous shortcuts in handling the deadly explosives. Harrison was one of six original members of his thirteen-man squad to survive unhurt the outfit's six months in the front line. In the remaining seven slots more than twenty men, one of whom was critically wounded before anyone had learned his name. Most of the engineer's losses came from German artillery rather than from mishandled mines. Aware of the sites where the engineers might erect temporary Bailey bridges, the German gunners kept these vital river crossings "zeroed in."

On December 16 a completely unforeseen massive German counteroffensive irrupted from the supposedly inactive Ardennes Forest. The Germans confounded the Anglo-American planning and intelligence staffs, who had not dreamed that the Nazis still possessed the strength for a major attack. The Battle of the Bulge raged on until late January, drawing in directly or indirectly every combat unit of Eisenhower's armies. Much of the dramatic story of the battle lay in countless holding actions by American small units at key points on both sides of the Bulge. By limiting the enemy penetration to the narrowest possible front, the American commanders sought to deny the Germans room necessary to generate offensive power. Thus the 1st Division was rushed to join the 2d and the 99th in defending the Elsenborn Ridge, a vital eminence on the north shoulder of the Bulge. While the battle was at its most desperate Walter Hillenmeyer had occasion to visit the headquarters of Lt. Gen. Courtney H. Hodges's First Army. It appeared to Hillenmeyer that Hodges's staff was more shaken by the German offensive than were the officers and men of the Big Red One whom he had just left at the front.

To permit the massing of reserves for a counterattack, the Allied lines north and south of the Bulge were thinned. Fortifying the lightly held sector of the 104th Division north of the main battlefield, Lowell Harrison and his fellow engineers planted hundreds of antitank mines. Often it was possible only to place the mines in the snow above the hard-frozen earth. Passing back through the division's picket lines, the engineers had to identify themselves to apprehensive, trigger-happy infantrymen who demanded whispered answers to trivia questions that no German infiltrator could have answered. One of the stumpers was, "Who plays shortstop for the Brooklyn Dodgers?" (The expected answer, of course, was Kentuckian Harold "Pee Wee" Reese, who was then in the navy.)

South of the salient General Patton redirected much of his Third Army northward into a full-scale battle on the underside of the Bulge. Patton's fifty- to seventy-five-mile redeployment of his immense command was an amazing administrative and logistical achievement. His 4th Armored Division battled through to the vital crossroads town of Bastogne, Belgium, which for some days had been defended by the surrounded 101st Airborne. To the 6th Armored fell the costly task of widening the narrow corridor initially opened by the 4th. In the midst of the battle the force of a nearby shell explosion hurled Embry Lagrew to the ground from the turret of his Sherman tank. Cracked vertebrae from the fall confined him to the hospital for an extended period after the war. Until V-E Day, however, regular injections of novacaine from a surgeon and nightly massages by a medic kept Lagrew in harness.

From the Ninth Army sector the powerful 2d Armored (with

many more tanks than divisions organized later on) was among several units shifted southward to the Bulge. On Christmas Day the Hell on Wheels struck the German spearhead head on, stemming the Nazi drive. A few days later the American tankers sideslipped to the left and attacked the northern side of the Bulge. The division's experience in the harsh winter battling bore out Chester Mercer's contention that a soldier who could somehow survive his first three weeks of combat had at least "a chance" to get through the war. Experience gave a man an instinctive sixth sense of impending danger. Mercer's armored-infantry platoon received thirty-eight green replacements just before being ordered to clean out a German pocket of resistance regardless of losses. Three days' fighting made casualties of every one of the thirty-eight.

At one point in the Battle of the Bulge, Mercer's men had secured an objective when Chester noticed the absence of his best friend, a man with whom for more than two years he had shared puptents and foxholes. Mercer trudged back more than a mile through heavy snow. Pee Wee, his friend, had been hit in both legs. The medics had somehow missed him, and he would have bled to death had Mercer not come searching. The wounded man weighed only 145 pounds, but he was nevertheless a very heavy burden to carry through the snow. Though Mercer learned later that Pee Wee had survived, he never saw or heard directly from his friend again. While together the two had been "closer than brothers." As Mercer later commented, "That's the way of soldiers." One makes friends quickly, then moves on to new ones.

Defeat in the Bulge finished the German offensively, but they continued to resist fiercely the slow Allied push to the Rhine. On 7 March 1945, however, First Army troops at Remagen luckily snatched from under the noses of the Germans a damaged railroad bridge across the great river. The First massed several divisions on the eastern bank in anticipation of a decisive breakout to the heart of Germany. An artillery spotter flying a Cub, Kentuckian Maj. James Townsend was the very first pilot to make a hazardous landing in the forward lodgment. And on March 11 vehicles began rolling across a floating treadway built under fire in just thirty-two hours by the 291st Engineer Combat Battalion, in which Henry Giles of Adair County was a sergeant. Later married to the author Janice Holt Giles, Henry stood watching as the original and badly damaged Ludendorff Bridge unexpectedly collapsed on March 17: "Was at my post as usual, about a hundred yards downstream, when there was this screeching, cracking, splintering noise. I looked over at the bridge & right before my eyes it began buckling & caving in. . . . It just collapsed. Sort of slow motion at first . . . then it began settling very fast."

East of the Rhine the Ninth and First Armies encircled more than three hundred thousand German troops in the heavily industrialized Ruhr Valley. That left nothing to prevent the victorious Americans from bolting ahead all the way to the Elbe River. The 30th and 2d Armored Divisions both drove forward with the vanguard of the Ninth Army. "Our troops are about 75 miles from Berlin tonight," exalted Harry Jackson on April 11. "This is an exciting and tragic time—We are going on and on—to Berlin."

Two bridgeheads were thrown across the Elbe. One of them turned out to be a hornets' nest for the 2d Armored Division. Falling hot fragments from air-bursting German antiaircraft shells peppered the American infantry on the eastern bank, rendering it impossible to bring the tanks across. A German attack drove the unsupported GIs back to the river, over which their evacuation was covered by the division's artillery. Chester Mercer recalled the loud insistence by an American colonel in the bridgehead that the humiliating retreat be conducted without undue haste. Without breaking stride, Mercer shouted agreement. The colonel kept pace all the way to the rear.

Despite the setback, the Ninth Army remained confident that Berlin lay within easy reach. But orders arrived on April 15 to hold in place on the Elbe-Mulde line. Most of Eisenhower's troops were to spend the last three weeks of the war awaiting the westward surge of the Soviet tide. The halt was probably wise. The western Allies had already taken possession of their assigned postwar zones of occupation. A thrust to Berlin might have collided with the Red Army. Moreover, as William Buster points out, the Allied armies were "strung out all over hell" after their recent spectacular advances.

During the interim before the German surrender on May 7,

thousands of German troops sought to give themselves up to the British and Americans. Lowell Harrison recalls that it was a nuisance to disarm and confine the countless Germans walking and crawling across a shattered bridge over the Mulde. A high percentage of the captives were boys and middle-aged men. American troops far out in front of their supplies were much more interested in scrounging for food and souvenirs. The imaginative scavengers quickly discovered that German families invariably concealed sausages, cheese, and other delectables in their ovens. Using local town criers, which many German villages still had in the 1940s, the Americans directed that all weapons (prized automatic pistols, especially) and binoculars be handed over to the visitors. According to Harrison, the GIs were gratified by the response of German civilians long accustomed to obeying orders.

The collapse of the Third Reich meant that the German people would have to accommodate themselves to their conquerors. Harry Jackson's first contacts back during the winter had impressed him with "the German's inability to understand our Democratic ways—He invariably misconstrues that for weakness, indecision, lack of discipline and a general disregard for law and order." And the owner of a captured German brewery appeared shocked to find that Embry Lagrew would sample beer in the company of enlisted men under his command.

But the Americans were infinitely more aghast over the atrocities they uncovered in Germany. Near Altenburg, Lagrew's armored combat command found several hundred Jewish women confined in two large buildings. Starvation had made living skeletons of the women. Sickened by the sight, Lagrew angrily ordered the staff of a nearby German hospital to care for the tragic victims, but many died in spite of the German doctors' best efforts. A few days after the German surrender, Harry Jackson visited a slave labor camp, and in June he inspected the site of the former "Buchenwald Prison Camp. . . . The horror and inhuman brutality of the SS guards is completely beyond my comprehension. There were some sixty-thousand prisoners herded into the barbed wire enclosure which covered about five acres. . . . I saw the crematorium and the death chamber where the prisoners were hung by the neck to a hook in the wall and beaten to death. . . . I cannot begin to describe the all-pervading terror that lingers within the camp even yet. Time will never eradicate the sadism that has been perpetrated behind those tragic walls, nor will it erase the guilt from the foul conduct of the German blackguards and murderers."

In retribution for Nazi Germany's crimes against humanity, a special Allied tribunal brought to justice at Nuremburg during 1945–46 some twenty-one surviving top-level leaders of the Third Reich. Guarding the prisoners in the dock was a detachment of American soldiers under Lt. Paul Foster of Glasgow, Kentucky. Foster had no trouble with Adolf Hitler's leading henchmen. His most embarassing moment at the trials resulted from the accidental firing of the pistol of a courtroom spectator—a military-police officer from whose gun Foster was removing the bullets before allowing him into the courtroom. To Foster's chagrin, a newswoman loudly insisted that the lieutenant had killed one of the defendants and concealed his body.

Widespread revulsion over Nazi war crimes did not long prevent the victors from ignoring stern prohibitions against fraternization with the German populace. Simon Lagrew found that rape was not much of a disciplinary problem; his soldiers had little difficulty in finding acquiescent women. By the end of July 1945 Harry Jackson was describing the Germans as "friendly," although "hostile to our occupation. I am sure I would be equally as hostile if the situation were reversed." It was hard to suppress all sympathy for the inhabitants of a country shattered by aerial bombardment. "Munich was a wonderful city before it was destroyed and so was Nuremburg," noted Jackson, "but they are now both lying in ruins. . . . There is nothing quite so appalling as a city of well over 800,000 inhabitants destroyed. There is a pall that sets over such places. . . . The whole scene is fearful." Yet Jackson shrewdly anticipated that the Germans would recover quickly from their overwhelming defeat. From Grenoble, France, in September he commented that "from what I have seen, if we gave Germany another ten years to rearm she would have France conquered again and with little trouble. The German is a very energetic man and has the faculty for organizing. They work like trojans."

More than anything else, the rapid abatement of Anglo-American antipathy toward the Germans was due to a pervasive chill cast by the collapse of the wartime alliance of convenience with the Soviet Union. British and American sea and air contributions to victory had far surpassed those of Russia, but the large-scale ground battles in the West during 1944–45 were dwarfed in duration and magnitude by the stupendous four-year struggle on the Eastern Frònt. Without the combined efforts of all three of the Allies, Germany would have been almost impossible to beat.

The first contacts between the Allied armies of the East and West made at least some American soldiers skeptical about Soviet goodwill toward the democracies. According to Lowell Harrison, there were about two days of visiting and souvenir-swapping after the Russians finally reached the eastern bank of the Mulde River. Of course, the language barrier rendered difficult any fraternizing much beyond simple handshaking and backslapping. The exchange of visits soon stopped, and across the river Russians could be seen digging machine-gun emplacements. Farther south, at Mitweiler, Simon Lagrew concluded that the Russians were the "god-damndest," most "vulgar" military force he had encountered. Lagrew's men once fired some shots at a Russian truck which plowed through an American roadblock, but no international complications arose from the incident.

For the moment, portents of the impending Cold War between the western Allies and the Soviet Union had to be ignored. On the opposite side of the world another war remained to be won.

4

AVENGERS OF BATAAN

ON V-E DAY few Americans had any reason to know that Japan would surrender within four months—before the first invading Allied soldier had touched Japanese soil. Even discerning military analysts expected final victory in the Far East to require massive reinforcements from Eisenhower's armies, plus help from the Soviet Union. Russia had promised in February 1945 to enter the war against Japan about three months after the surrender of Germany. Shortly after May 7, certain American units and higher headquarters staffs returned home from Europe in anticipation of early reassignment to the Pacific. High on the list of divisions to be redeployed were such formations as the 104th—thoroughly seasoned but still "young" in comparison to such veteran outfits as the Big Red One, which remained behind. Their home furloughs over by August, Lowell Harrison and other men of the 104th learned to use flamethrowers, which for some unexplained reason they had not employed against the Germans. Before the massive transfer of veterans of the German conflict was very far along, the Japanese surrender brought it to a halt. Had the war lasted, the reinforcements from Europe would have fought in March 1946 in the invasion of Honshu, the principal Japanese home island.

Ground combat in the Pacific had been comparatively small in scale. But the struggle against Japan placed heavy demands upon the American naval and air arms. And the very vastness of the Pacific posed staggering logistical challenges for Allied planners. The relative shortage of available American troops, and ships to carry them, was undoubtedly a blessing in disguise—American strategists were forced to exploit their air and naval superiority and bypass numerous heavily defended Japanese-held islands. Had more troops been available, the temptation to find battles for them to fight would have been irresistible.

The United States grasped the initiative in the Pacific six months after Pearl Harbor. The June 1942 victory at Midway in the Central Pacific gave America a rough naval parity with Japan. The equilibrium prevailed until the second half of 1943, when the full flood of men and matériel massed by the American mobilization began pouring into the battle zones. Yet the United States had not waited for the completion of vessels in shipyards or for the deployment of divisions and aerial squadrons still in training. As early as 7 August 1942 the 1st Marine Division invaded Guadalcanal in the Solomon Islands of the South Pacific. Adm. Ernest J. King, professional head of the American navy, had insisted that the United States seize Guadalcanal before planes from a Japanese airbase under construction there struck at the vulnerable shipping lanes from America to Australia. For six long months, while both sides threw in reinforcements, a desperate battle raged for possession of the malarial, jungle-covered island and its surrounding waters. From August through November 1942 there were six fierce naval battles in the Slot—the waters between the parallel island chains of the Solomon group. Domination of the Slot was certain to bring eventual control of Guadalcanal.

The pivotal naval clash, the second Battle of Guadalcanal, was fought and won in the night of 14–15 November 1942 by an American task force formed around the new battleships *Washington* and *South Dakota,* and under the command of Rear Adm. Willis A. "Ching" Lee, Jr., of Owenton, Kentucky. Just two nights earlier in the wild melee of the first Battle of Guadalcanal the United States had lost two cruisers, each with a rear admiral. In partial compensation, the American navy had managed to disrupt an attempted Japanese bombardment of the troops on shore.

Now, once again, the enemy meant to strike at the exposed American defensive perimeter and its priceless airfield. The gravity of the Japanese threat justified exposing the precious American battleships in the confined waters of Ironbottom Sound. Screened by four destroyers, Lee's battleships steamed westward between Guadalcanal and Savo islands. In a disastrous destroyer duel several thousand yards ahead, two of the escorts were sunk. But Lee's capital ships plowed forward through the wreckage. From the battleships men threw life preservers to swimming survivors of the lost tin cans. A critical electrical power failure suddenly rendered the *South Dakota* helpless, and fire from a pair of enemy heavy cruisers punished her terribly. In the meantime, blips on the radar screen of the *Washington,* Lee's flagship, betrayed the whereabouts of the Japanese battlewagon *Kirishima.* So accurate was the fire of the *Washington's* five- and sixteen-inch guns that the *Kirishima* had to be scuttled. Then, with long-range fire, the *Washington* drove the two Japanese cruisers away from the *South Dakota*.

The victory established American naval ascendancy at Guadalcanal and was hailed by President Roosevelt as a "turning-point in this war." The maritime historian Samuel Eliot Morison declared that "from 15 November 1942 until 15 August 1945 the war followed the right fork. It was rough, tough and uncharted, but it led to Tokyo."

The capable, unpretentious Willis Lee continued on sea duty for most of the war. Promoted to vice-admiral in 1944, he commanded the fast battleships of Adm. Raymond A. Spruance's Fifth Fleet. Described by Morison as "an officer of alert mind and keen analytical sense, whose advice was often sought on strategy," Lee shouldered command responsibilities parallel to those of Vice-Adms. Marc A. Mitscher (fast carriers) and Richmond Kelly Turner (amphibious forces). But he was little known outside the service. His battleships had been replaced by aircraft carriers as the navy's primary offensive weapons. Most naval fleet missions in the Central Pacific were air strikes against Japanese-held islands, so Mitscher normally exercised tactical command under the overall direction of Spruance, or, alternatively, of Adm. William F. Halsey, Jr. Lee's battlewagons accompanied the carriers and shielded them with antiaircraft fire. In the unlikely event of a classic Trafalgar-type surface battle between the battle lines of the American and Japanese navies, Lee would have assumed tactical command. In the air age, any such battle would necessarily have taken place at night. The prudent Spruance saw no reason to hazard a night battle when he could safely base his strategy upon the unquestioned daylight superiority of Mitscher's fliers over the enemy.

It was Halsey's misdirected superaggressiveness at Leyte Gulf that aborted Lee's only opportunity to fight the climactic surface battle of the century. On 20 October 1944 a massive armada composed of Halsey's Third and Adm. Thomas C. Kinkaid's Seventh fleets had returned General MacArthur to the Philippines to begin the ten-month-long air, sea, and ground campaign for the liberation of the archipelago. In response, the Imperial Japanese Fleet sallied forth in its last fruitless attempt to regain command of the seas from the Americans. Appalling attrition among naval aviators had long since taken most of the bite from Japan's aircraft carriers, but the battleships of the enemy fleet were still formidable. Courting disaster, Admiral Halsey set out in hot pursuit of a decoy force of toothless carriers, leaving the exposed invasion beaches on Leyte's eastern shore vulnerable to the unanticipated approach of a separate task force of Japanese battleships. Having deduced that the Japanese carrier group was merely bait, Admiral Lee urged Halsey to form Task Force 34 (the battle line) and leave it under Lee's command to shield MacArthur's beaches. The fleet commander ignored Lee's wise counsel, and left the defense of the lodgment to the small escort carriers and destroyers of the Seventh Fleet. With Halsey's capital ships far away in the early morning hours of October 25, Admiral Kurita's battleships had a splendid opportunity to devastate Leyte's naked beaches. But a fierce delaying action by the American destroyers and "jeep" carriers caused Kurita to lose heart. Instead of pressing ahead, the Japanese admiral reversed his course, easily making good his escape from Halsey's distant fleet. The Japanese fleet never again challenged the American navy. Still, given the chance to form Task Force 34 at Leyte, Admiral Lee might well have finished off the Japanese battle line.

As a rifleman Willis Lee had won an Olympic medal in 1920. In naval gunnery and antiaircraft defense, he was a pioneer in the use of radar detection, a technical field in which he had made himself an expert. His weather-beaten face made Admiral Lee appear older than his fifty-seven years, but in fact the long stretches of wartime sea duty had taken their toll by 1945. Off Okinawa in April and May of that year Lee's battleships bore the principal burden of covering with antiaircraft fire the ships of Spruance's Fifth Fleet from the relentless attacks of Japanese kamikazes—suicidal pilots who deliberately crashed their planes into American and British ships. Rotated home at the end of May with the other Fifth Fleet commanders, Lee succumbed only three months later to a fatal heart seizure.

From Guadalcanal to Okinawa the three-year advance of American surface and ground forces could be charted by armchair strategists back home. But beneath the seas there was another war, a "silent" struggle which was impossible to plot because ordinary citizens knew very little about it. Comprising only 2 percent of the United States Navy, the submarine force nevertheless sank 55 percent of all Japanese maritime tonnage destroyed during the war. Submarine service was hazardous; 22 percent of all war-patrol participants were eventually lost. But even during the catastrophic early months of the conflict "pig boats" stalked the coasts of Japan itself. Had they not been rendered ineffective during the initial stages of the conflict by defective torpedoes, the submarine might have made a favorable impact on the fighting as early as 1942. Not until September 1943 were all of the problems of the "dud" torpedoes finally resolved, but over the last two years of the war American submarines strangled Japan with an ever-tighter blockade.

One of the top submarines in the Pacific was the U.S.S. *Silversides*, commanded on its first five patrols by Lt. Cdr. Creed C. Burlingame of Louisville. In his late thirties, Burlingame was older than most of the skippers of the Silent Service. Unlike many of his cautious contemporaries, he was a risk-taking fatalist without apparent fear of senior officers on shore or enemy vessels at sea. At a dance in Australia he once inquired of a major general wearing cavalry pants and boots the whereabouts of the man's horse. Annoyed, the general asked in response the location of Burlingame's ship. "My ship has been a hell of a lot closer to Japan than your horse has," shot back Burlingame.

Shortly after his graduation from Annapolis, Burlingame had applied for training as a submariner. Even as a midshipman he had been intensely interested in the small but potentially deadly boats. He found appealing the close, friendly atmosphere among their crews. Of course there was no place aboard such a crowded vessel for any man lacking the ability to work harmoniously with others. By the time Burlingame commissioned the *Silversides* just eight days after Pearl Harbor, he had completed more than a decade with the Silent Service.

In April 1942 Burlingame took the *Silversides* on her first wartime patrol—a fifty-five-day mission to the Japanese coast. "We went out blind as mice," he recalls ruefully. The boat's radar rarely worked, and when it did it identified only aerial objects. Even then, it could not identify or give the direction or range of aircraft. To attack effectively at that stage of the war, the *Silversides* needed daylight. Burlingame had to line up his targets by periscope, a sighting device that left a betraying wake on the surface. A forewarned ship could outrun the submerged American pig boat. Burlingame contends that the spectacular upward curve of kills by American submarines later in the war owed much to the introduction of surface radar, which allowed the aiming of a submerged boat without the use of its periscope, and which worked with equal proficiency in daytime or darkness.

Depth-chargings by enemy destroyers were what submariners dreaded most. The wartime chronicler of the *Silversides* likened the experience to hearing first a "mysterious click," then a "dreadful crash," and finally "the strange, metallic rumble of water through the superstructure,'" all of which could last for hours if the destroyers were persistent. But "there was no sense worrying about it," declares Burlingame, who endured numerous depth-chargings during his five patrols. As captain it was essential to appear cool in the grimmest of times. Not conventionally religious, Burlingame worked off his tensions by rubbing the belly of a "lucky" bronze Buddha in the conning tower. Other Buddhas were placed in the forward and aft torpedo chambers. A depth-charging once kept Burlingame busily rubbing away for six hours. Preoccupied, he gave little thought to the sharp navel in Buddha's belly. The crisis over, he was dumbstruck to discover on the deck a pool of blood from his lacerated thumb, an incident which "amused hell out of the crew."

Burlingame's fourth patrol, early in 1943, turned out to be his most hectic, as well as one of the most remunerative of the entire war. Only a few days out of Brisbane, Australia, a crew member suffered an attack of acute appendicitis; the appendix was successfully removed by the boat's pharmacist's mate. North of Truk the *Silversides* sank a ten-thousand-ton enemy tanker, a score at least as valuable to the overwall American war effort as a light cruiser would have been. Meeting a convoy, Burlingame sank three freighters with five torpedoes, all of them hits. Later, on the surface, he was horrified to discover that a sixth torpedo had failed to fire and was hanging half-way out of its tube. There was no way to defuse the torpedo's warhead. Vigorously rubbing Buddha's belly and running the submarine's diesels at full reverse speed, Burlingame ordered the deadly torpedo refired. This time it cleared the tube and streaked away.

The cramped and perilous life of a submariner had its rewards. It was a "rather clean war," says Burlingame. The men of a pig boat lived and (if need be) died all together—no one had to watch as one by one the mangled bodies of old friends were carried away. Submariners' food was the "best in the navy," but few men put on excess weight because the simple act of moving around a crowded boat was "an acrobatic feat." And between patrols crewmen enjoyed two weeks' free time in Honolulu or Australia. Early in the war the navy had leased the famed Royal Hawaiian Hotel on Waikiki Beach to provide a rest and recreational haven for submariners. One of Burlingame's long-lingering memories is the sight of navy "skivvies" hanging out to dry in the windows of the plush hotel.

That the submarine force was fighting a different war from the rest of the navy was plain enough to Kenneth M. Carr, a native of Mayfield, Kentucky, and in 1943–44 an enlisted landing-craft crewman in the Solomon Islands. In the evenings during slack periods Carr often watched in fascination as submarines came purring on one diesel into Purvis Bay—as stealthily as cat-burglars. Lying low in the water, a submarine resembled nothing so much as "a giant snake." Like other surface sailors of the era, Carr was told very little of the vital role being played in the war by the Silent Service.

While the submarines waged their protracted war of attrition, a two-pronged American offensive moved inexorably closer to Japan. By late 1943 the Joint Chiefs of Staff and the Pacific commanders had refined their famous island-hopping strategy. Whenever possible, Japanese strongpoints were to be bypassed and their defenders left to wither on the vine. With aircraft carriers it became possible by 1944 to assault islands well beyond the range of land-based airplanes. Indeed, the purpose of most Pacific landings was the seizure of strategic sites for airfields from which to dominate the surrounding waters and neighboring islands.

Traditionally, ship-to-shore attacks had been universally acknowledged as the most difficult of military operations. Before World War II amphibious landings normally succeeded only against the feeblest of defenses. In the 1930s, though, the increasing probability of a Pacific war had persuaded both the Japanese and American navies to develop the specialized equipment and combat doctrines needed for amphibious assaults.

The operators of landing craft were mostly wartime personnel. Without permanent assignment to a particular ship, they continually made runs to the beachhead as various transports arrived, unloaded, and departed. Ensign John Minton commanded a landing unit of as many as eight LCMs (Landing Craft, Mechanized): steel-hulled, ramp-dropping boats powered by two marine diesel engines and capable of putting ashore 108 infantrymen or a light tank. To avoid damage, the boats rode over coral reefs on ocean swells. By catching breaking waves, the boats could get themselves well on shore. Minton found that seventeen- and eighteen-year-old lads who did not spare their engines made the best boatmen. The Kentuckian's only amphibious assault was one of the bitterest battles of the war: the capture of Peleliu in the Palau archipelago during the fall of 1944. An objective that the 1st Marine Division expected to take in a mere three days required instead a full three months and the help of the army's 81st Division. Even worse, the battle appears to have been unnecessary. Knowledgeable students have concluded that Peleliu could safely have been bypassed.

Over the first couple of days' fighting, Minton's boats plied back and forth from the ships to a transfer point some three hundred yards offshore. Making the final approach to the beach were amphibious tractors capable of running over the reefs and crawling on land. Among Minton's passengers was a burial detachment carrying crosses and Star of David grave markers. Back to the transports his unit evacuated an unceasing stream of wounded marines. Many were no older than nineteen or twenty. Some were dazed with shell shock, while others tried gamely to make light of their misery. Minton recalls one lad who had lost an arm and who said, "You can just call me 'Lefty' from now on." A number of the wounded men subsequently died and were buried at sea.

Once the beachhead was firmly established, Minton's boats hauled cargo ashore. Provisions were disgorged from the transports in the exact reverse of the order in which they had been combat loaded according to a meticulous schedule. Boatmen prized top-priority medical supplies, which were always immediately waved in by the beachmasters. Ammunition was also accepted and unloaded promptly, but the LCMs might have to drift for hours with diesel fuel or packing timber. Eventually, of course, dunnage from the ships would be used as construction material. Unloaded, the ship to which Minton's unit had been attached sailed away. On their own, he and his crewmen lived in their LCMs, frequently lashing two or three together to allow most of the sailors to rest while their boats drifted. Minton especially remembers drifting on one occasion with three boatloads of 155-millimeter shells. His sailors gave no outward sign of worry that a single direct hit from a Japanese gun on Peleliu would instantly have destroyed all three boats. No spot on shore was entirely safe either, Minton recalls. Once, while standing in a chow line, he saw a man a few places ahead of him suddenly fall to the ground. He had been cut down by a concealed enemy sniper.

In contrast to almost-forgotten Peleliu, Iwo Jima, conquered in February and March of 1945, quickly established itself in the American folk tradition. At terrible cost three marine divisions seized the small volcanic island halfway between Saipan and Tokyo. As a fighter-plane base, weather station, and emergency landing field, Iwo Jima was later to save the lives of several thousand of the American bomber crewmen based in the Marianas and regularly attacking Japan. From Iwo came an enduring symbol of the "uncommon valor" of the Marine Corps: the famous Joe Rosenthal photograph of the flag-raising on top of Mount Suribachi. Second from the left among the six marines in Rosenthal's picture is Pfc. Franklin R. Sousley of Ewing, Kentucky. To his family Sousley wrote that "the hill was hard and I sure never expected war to be like it was those first four days. I got some [bullet rips] through my clothing, and I sure am happy that I am still O.K. At least four slant-eyed Japs will never see TOKYO again." Nor did Sousley survive the battle. He was killed on March 12, one of three men in Rosenthal's photograph to die on Iwo Jima.

In the midst of the agonizing drive northward from Mount Suribachi to clear the remainder of Iwo Jima, Kentuckian William Barber spotted the distant flag to his rear. The sight of the colors on the morning they were hoisted carried a "special brand of exhilaration." A platoon commander in the 5th Marine Division, Barber and his comrades had never harbored any illusions about the likely tenacity of the Japanese defenders, but like most marines Barber had great confidence in the training, weapons, and combat techniques of the corps.

Even during wartime the Marine Corps was composed mostly of volunteers, and its ranks contained a higher percentage of regulars than the army had. The marines' comparatively small numbers and offensive mission led them to regard their corps as the elite branch of the American armed forces. As amphibious-assault troops the marines conducted short, intense campaigns. Vulnerable ships could not be tied to the support of ground operations without risk to themselves, so the marines' tactical doctrine emphasized winning battles swiftly. In contrast, the army, with a mission of conducting large-scale and protracted ground fighting, followed a much more methodical, conservative combat doctrine.

Iwo Jima had appeared strangely quiet to Barber when he caught his first glimpse of the island at dawn on 19 February 1945 (D Day). From his ship he could see "occasional puffs" of dust raised by shells and aerial bombs. In LCVPs (Landing Craft, Vehicle Personnel) Barber's platoon waited offshore with the 5th Division's reserves. By that stage of the war the Japanese had learned not to contest at the water's edge an American landing backed by naval gunfire. But there was "fire on us" from the moment Barber led his men ashore. For marines and vehicles alike, Iwo Jima's loose volcanic surface rendered difficult the simple act of solidly planting feet or treads. On the barren island the days were hot and the nights chilly, but there was little rainfall to foul rifle barrels.

It was, of course, impossible for the Japanese to reinforce the eight-square-mile flyspeck in the Pacific Ocean. On Iwo Jima tanks would have availed the defenders but little, as no spot on the island was outside the range of the navy's sixteen-inch guns. Nevertheless, fighting mostly with small arms, the heavily outnumbered Japanese exacted a fearful toll from the invaders. Dug into bunkers and caves, they refused to surrender. Somehow, the American marines drove unrelentingly forward, firing rifles, machine guns, and artillery. With flamethrowers, mortars, bazookas, grenades, and satchel charges they blasted pillboxes and sealed the mouths of caves. Unfortunately, however, the caverns usually had more than one opening.

Before his initial combat on Iwo Jima, the war had seemed to William Barber a "somewhat impersonal" matter. But after witnessing the deaths of friends, he "hated" the Japanese; they were "as much of an enemy as I can ever imagine having." Like a "western shoot-out," this battle, especially, confronted its participants with the harsh alternatives of killing or being killed. Passion and danger aroused recklessness among several of Barber's men. He had to restrain two or three from running foolhardy risks. In common with military leaders from squads to the highest echelons of command, Barber found that his responsibilities as platoon commander kept him too busy to feel fear in combat or boredom behind the lines.

From dawn to dusk day after day the marines edged forward, often bypassing enemy strong points in the process. The Americans had been trained to advance at night, but they wisely chose to exploit the Japanese proclivity for infiltrating and counterattacking under a cloak of darkness. From their two-man nighttime foxholes the marines inflicted heavy losses upon enemies who rarely exposed themselves in daylight. Barber found that the unslackening pace of the campaign pushed men to the limits of their endurance. In battle, he concedes, the "fatigue eventually does sort of numb you," but the youthful and resiliant marines of Iwo Jima drew upon "all sorts of second winds and second reservoirs" of energy. Like so many of his comrades Barber was wounded. A bullet which grazed his hand as he was reaching for a grenade did not force him out of the battle, but a couple of days afterward as his outfit prepared for a dawn jump-off Barber was stunned by the blast of a nearby, and rare, Japanese shell. Apparently unhurt, he soon coughed up blood from internal hemorrhaging caused by the shock of the concussion. It was, he has insisted, the sort of wound that sounds much worse than it really is. Evacuated by sea to Guam, Barber soon encountered in the hospital the badly wounded commander of his company. Realizing at once that "I belonged on Iwo," Barber flew back and led the company through the final stages of the battle.

So far as Admiral Spruance's Fifth Fleet was concerned, Iwo Jima and Okinawa were successive phases of the same campaign. By March 16, when organized resistance ended on Iwo Jima, the naval and air preliminaries of the invasion of Okinawa were well under way. The United States meant to gain there a ground-forces staging area, a fleet anchorage, and airbases for fighters and medium bombers, all for a possible invasion of Japan, only 350 miles to the north. Moreover, Okinawa would complete a chain of American bases necessary to choke the island empire with a naval blockade. "A limited land mass" in military jargon, the sixty-mile-long island would require an amphibious assault, followed by an extended land battle. Until it was over, a huge Anglo-American fleet would remain offshore and subject to air attacks from Japan.

The designated Okinawa landing force was the Tenth Army, three marine and four army divisions under the army's Lt. Gen. Simon B. Buckner, Jr., of Munfordville, Kentucky. Smaller than his erect bearing and large chest made him appear, the fifty-eight-year-old silver-haired soldier was the son of a Confederate general and Kentucky governor. Buckner had spent most of the war in the remote Alaskan theater, where he had proven himself a hard-driving administrator and builder of airfields—and a man of dogmatic opinions. Following the capture of Attu in the Aleutians, Buckner proclaimed that the Japanese preference for suicide over surrender "shows that the Jap, at heart, is a quitter"! Shortly after Pearl Harbor, Buckner had ordered the detention of every Japanese resident in the Alaska Defense Command area. To one family anxious to retain a trusted servant, he insisted that "the only Japanese who can harm us are those we trust." Buckner's well-publicized enthusiasm for "killing Japs" ("yellow termites") was similar to the posturing of the navy's colorful Admiral Halsey. Professionally, the career-infantryman Buckner's Alaskan experiences had made him unusually knowledgeable about the potentialities and limitations of military aviation. But he had far less understanding of the realities of naval warfare.

The summer of 1944 had marginally embroiled the blunt, but likeable, Buckner in the bitterest interservice dispute of the war. On Saipan, the commander of the army's lackluster 27th Division was removed upon the insistence of the marines' Lt. Gen. Holland M. Smith, the landing-force commander in the invasion. The decision infuriated the senior army officer in the Central Pacific theater, Lt. Gen. Robert C. Richardson, Jr., who had long maintained that an army general should have led the Saipan fighting instead of Smith. Richardson formed a board of inquiry under General Buckner. That Buckner's board found the dismissal of the army's Ralph Smith to have been unwarranted amounted to a directed verdict in view of Richardson's vehement opinion that no marine general was fit to command any formation higher than a division. A battlefield commander's right to remove an unsatisfactory subordinate is not normally open to question, but, prizing harmony in his Pacific command, Adm. Chester W. Nimitz did not again place army troops under the marines' Holland Smith—which cleared the way for Buckner to command the Okinawa invasion.

Buckner's generalship at Okinawa received mixed reviews. Still green as a field commander, and at a very late stage of the war, he faced a formidable task. Buckner won the personal esteem of subordinates by his approachability, bravery, and unquestioned determination to push the battle to a victorious conclusion. Tactful men, Admirals Nimitz and Spruance were loathe to second-guess Buckner's preference during the campaign for orthodox frontal attacks against the well-entrenched Japanese. But during a visit by the theater commander to Okinawa, Buckner nettled Nimitz by declaring roundly that ground operations were none of the navy's concern. At the time, Buckner's advance was stalled and Spruance's supporting ships were desperately fending off kamikazes. Nimitz left Buckner in no uncertainty that he would be replaced in command of the Tenth Army unless there was forward progress within four days. A less forbearing critic of Buckner than Nimitz or Spruance was the commandant of the Marine Corps, Gen. A.A. Vandegrift, who chafed throughout the campaign over what he regarded as Buckner's unduly conservative methods. With the tacit consent of Admiral King, Vandegrift publicly deplored through the syndicated columnist David Lawrence the failure of General Buckner to expedite the campaign by staging a second landing in the Japanese rear. Buckner had long since rejected the idea, contending that it was logistically "impracticable." Vandegrift responded that the prolonged campaign had cost more lives than would have been lost had Buckner been willing to gamble. The official Marine Corps campaign history refrains from belaboring Buckner over his failure to mount the attack. But interestingly enough, one of its advocates was the commander of the army's 77th Division, which with just such a maneuver had struck the decisive blow in the Leyte campaign.

Most of the fighting on Okinawa came some days after the initial landings about halfway up the island's west side on Easter Sunday, 1 April 1945. The majority of the Japanese defenders were massed to the south. On April 16, with a 6th Marine Division sweep to secure the northernmost part of Okinawa, Cpl. Richard E. Bush of Glasgow, Kentucky, suffered machine-gun wounds in both legs. Awaiting medical treatment, he spotted a rolling hand grenade. Instinctively, Bush covered the grenade with his helmet and his body, thus muffling its explosion. He survived, but with the loss of one eye, serious damage to the other, the deprivation of several fingers, and terrible burns. For his self-sacrifice, which undoubtedly saved the lives of several comrades, Bush became one of seven Kentuckians awarded the Medal of Honor during the Second World War.

By June the Tenth Army had worn down the enemy with frontal assaults, finally breaking the Japanese Shuri Line in southern

Okinawa. On the eighteenth victory was close at hand. At 1:15 that afternoon, observing an advance by the 8th Marine Regiment, General Buckner was struck in the chest by coral fragments sent flying by nearby shellbursts. He died within minutes, the highest ranking American combat fatality of the war. The general was laid to rest in the soil of the island his men had conquered. Four years later his remains were returned to Kentucky—to lie in Frankfort next to those of his father.

Some eight hundred miles southwest of Okinawa, the United States Sixth Army conducted from 9 January 1945 to the surrender of Japan a campaign that surpassed in magnitude any other American World War II land operation outside of northwestern Europe: the liberation of Luzon, largest of the Philippine Islands. The Joint Chiefs of Staff had concluded that the immense land mass was an unacceptable Japanese threat to the advancing American lines of communication. In American hands, Luzon would isolate the Japanese oil reserves in the Dutch East Indies and provide a huge base for staging the invasion of Japan, an operation which the War Department's planners persisted in regarding as a necessity for finishing the war. To defend Luzon were some 275,000 Japanese soldiers in three separate groups under the overall direction of General Yamashita.

With National Guardsmen from Kentucky and Indiana as its core, the 38th Division fought on Luzon from the end of January to the close of the war. The division's Kentucky components were the 149th Infantry Regiment and the 138th Field Artillery Battalion. The 38th had long been in federal service, but its first taste of combat had come only on the third anniversary of Pearl Harbor during the "mopping up" phase of the fighting on Leyte, where the division had been sent to stage for Luzon.

Heading the 1st Batallion of the 149th Regiment was Louisville's Lt. Col. Arthur C. Bonneycastle, a Kentucky National Guardsman since 1925. Roughly a third of his men were Kentuckians, but a fair number of the draftees who had fleshed out the ranks came from West Virginia and western Pennsylvania. Like the Kentuckians they were "good boys," their colonel fondly recalls. His men "were rough, but they'd stay with you." Of mostly rural origins, they were not necessarily expert marksmen but were much less prone than city dwellers would have been to waste ammunition. Back in the United States Bonneycastle's battalion had enjoyed the dubious distinction of a high venereal-disease rate, but in the tropics his men "were real good" about taking malaria tablets, realizing that it was a "take 'em or die" proposition.

Like the Japanese three years back, the Americans invaded Luzon at Lingayen Gulf. Three weeks later the 38th Division made an unopposed landing at a second beachhead on the China Sea. On shore a goateed "little white man" on a donkey hailed Colonel Bonneycastle by name. An American soldier, he had led guerrillas in the mountains of Luzon since the fall of Bataan, and had been alerted by radio to expect the landing.

The 38th swiftly drove south to Subic Bay, then eastward across the base of Bataan to seal off the peninsula from use by the Japanese as a last refuge. But the drive bogged down when the division ran into stiff resistence at "Zigzag Pass," a narrow, winding dirt road through the low hills east of Olongapo. With his 151st and 152d regiments stalled in the dense jungle terrain, Maj. Gen. H.L.C. Jones lost command of the division. His successor, cavalryman Brig. Gen. William C. Chase, had recently led a "flying column" on a spectacular end run from Lingayen to Manila. Chase later wrote that when he took over the 38th Division he had "had a great deal of service with our National Guard, and was most sympathetic with it. Some regular officers were not so inclined. . . . I felt at home . . . with these fine officers and men—but we had to get moving."

Chase promptly replaced several senior officers including Brig. Gen. Roy W. Easley, the assistant division commander and a politically active National Guardsman from Louisville. The relief of Easley occasioned no great stir in the division or back in Kentucky, although political storms had been raised earlier in the war by the removal of National Guard generals. The poor combat performance of several guard divisions had been due more to their early shipment overseas than to their militia background. Divisions sent abroad after the beginning of 1943—including those of the National Guard—had received thorough training in the United States and nearly always did well in battle. Despite its brief setback, the 38th under Chase was later to be one of three American divisions singled out for praise by General Yamashita. In short, the results more than justified the abrupt command shakeup at Zigzag Pass.

Chase took charge on February 7. Already, the 149th Infantry had begun the march that was to assure victory at the pass. Guided by spear-bearing Negrito pygmies, and carrying only packs, light weapons, and medical supplies, the 149th spent five agonizing days struggling on foot up a faint, mountainous trail some eight thousand yards to the north of the contested pass. Its flanking maneuver completed, the regiment attacked Zigzag from the rear. The 38th Division's vise crushed the Japanese defenders, killing some 1,846 of the enemy. Many of the dead could be attributed to the American artillery and to tactical air support. Phosphorous shells and napalm bombs had literally seared away tropical foliage, calling to mind a remark attributed earlier in the war to an apocryphal Japanese captive who declared that Americans did not fight in the jungles—they removed them. Masters of concealment though they were, the enemy could never hope to match with small arms, machine guns, and mortars the immense firepower of American cannon and aircraft. Throughout the Luzon campaign, Arthur Bonneycastle recalls, the P-38 Lockheed Lightenings of the Army Air Force did "outstandingly good" work in support of the infantry.

Less than one month after coming ashore, the 38th Division had cleared Bataan of organized opposition. On his outfit's shoulder patch, General Chase arranged to add the words "Avengers of Bataan." Up went a billboard boasting proudly, "You are now entering Bataan courtesy of 38th Infantry Division." At Zigzag Pass there was soon erected a stone marker commemorating the defense of the same ground in 1941-42 by the ill-starred National Guard tankers from Harrodsburg, Kentucky.

The 38th spent most of March and April annihilating the Japanese Kembu Group in the rugged Zambales Mountains. The painful sweep rated as nothing more than a mopping-up operation in the strategic "big picture." Hampering a forward progress was a shortage of ammunition, especially of 4.2-inch mortar rounds. Despite all obstacles, the attackers killed Japanese in wholesale lots. The totals beggar belief. On April 22, to cite one case, three brothers from Pike County, Kentucky, dispatched respectively seventeen, eighteen, and nineteen of the enemy, according to an Associated Press report. Sadly, one of the lads, Pfc. Edward Maynard, was felled by machine-gun fire and died in the arms of Edgar Maynard, his twin. Before the Zambales battling was done, the 38th Division reported slaying about eight thousand Japanese at a cost of 52 killed and 227 wounded. Throughout its eight-odd months in combat the division's losses were a modest 784 killed and 2,680 wounded, not especially low figures for the Southwest Pacific theater.

The amazing discrepancy between American and Japanese casualties on Luzon must have bewildered survivors of such hard-fought, but smaller-scale, Central Pacific battles as Peleliu and Iwo Jima. Iwo alone cost 6,821 American lives, and about three times that many Japanese. But on Luzon only 8,310 American ground troops were killed, as opposed to 205,535 Japanese. The 38th claimed some 26,469 kills, a figure which, if true, would account for an eighth of all the Japanese deaths during the campaign. Luckily for the Avengers of Bataan, the Luzon battling was vastly different from that of Peleliu or Iwo Jima. Luzon offered ample space for maneuver, especially after the Sixth Army had won Manila, Manila Bay, and the Central Luzon Plain. In their mountain retreats the Japanese could not hope to feed themselves off the country, and the American navy had sealed them off from reinforcements, medicine, ammunition (especially artillery shells), and gasoline. As time passed, the Japanese became sickly and malnourished—and thus emotionally apathetic. Death or, increasingly, capture became a release from an intolerable predicament. Filipino guerrillas were eager to help finish off their former, and cruel, oppressors. The early seizure on Luzon of bases for the Army Air Force afforded the luxury of cautious tactics; in contrast to Okinawa there was no need for vulnerable carriers to remain offshore.

By early March 1945 the Sixth Army held strategic control of Luzon, permitting conversion of the island into an enormous logistical base and staging area to get under way. Yet the Japanese remained for many weeks strong enough to threaten the build-up, so American troops continued to hammer away at the Kembu and

Shimbu groups to the west and east of Manila, and at the Shobu Group under General Yamashita's personal direction in northern Luzon. Yamashita meant to tie down the Sixth Army as long as possible. To his strategy of delay, wild banzai charges would have contributed nothing. Occasionally, the Japanese attempted to attack; more often they tried to infiltrate the American lines at night. But theirs was basically a strategy of passive defense. Yamashita successfully prolonged the Luzon campaign, but he failed to delay significantly the preparations for the invasion of Japan.

The nature of the fighting confronting the Americans in Philippine jungles is misrepresented by fat, black arrows on sketch-maps. Jungle or mountain battling actually involved many coordinated, but widely dispersed, small-unit engagements—not collisions of closely packed masses of men. In the march around Zigzag Pass and afterward, Arthur Bonneycastle's battalion operated largely out of the sight of other units. Often his infantrymen received supplies by air drop. Of course, it was usually easy to call in artillery or air support. At night the Americans dug themselves in. Anything moving during the hours of darkness was a "dead carabao, or a dead Filipino, or a dead Japanese." Incidents occurred that in retrospect are humorous. Bonneycastle especially remembers one junior officer making his usual early-morning visit to a nearby latrine. Seated there was a Japanese soldier who with his rifle promptly shot the American's carbine from his hands. The man hastened back to the battalion command post looking "sorta' whitish."

Over several days at the end of April, the 38th Division shuttled by truck eastward from the Zambales to the Sierra Madre on the far side of Manila. In the mountains the Japanese Shimbu Group held the Ipo Dam and the smaller, less important Wawa Dam, controlling thereby about half of Manila's water supply. Assisted by several aggressive medium tanks, two of which carried flamethrowers, the 149th Regiment captured the Wawa in late May. By the end of June the Shimbu Group was finished as an effective fighting force. At that stage of the campaign the battle-hardened 38th Division advanced with business-like efficiency—and with the support of prodigious firepower. Aircraft lavishly scorched hillsides with napalm. On the ground the infantry roasted out enemy bunkers with flamethrowers. Caves were blasted by ninety-millimeter antiaircraft cannon that fired directly into their mouths. At night the 38th discouraged would-be infiltrators or attackers by sweeping the terrain with surplus antiaircraft searchlights. Another important battlefield innovation was the evacuation of wounded men in bizarre aircraft that rose straight upward. These were called helicopters, the amazed GIs were told.

With the help of some ten thousand Filipino auxiliaries, the Avengers of Bataan spent the final weeks of the war cleaning out the Sierre Madre at a pace sufficiently relaxed to permit the rotation of battalions between the mountains and rest areas in the rear. There, weary soldiers enjoyed such diversions as a United Services Organization show staged by comedian Joe E. Brown. Appreciated even more than Brown's jokes were the chorus girls of his troupe. In the hills Japanese were proving so hard to find that General Chase threatened with mock-seriousness to impose strict quotas on the number that individual patrols could run down. At the end of the war disease and starvation were killing ten enemy soldiers for every one slain by the 38th and the Filipinos. Through the first twenty-eight days of July the division suffered only three battle deaths.

Indeed, by the late summer of 1945 the 38th like other Pacific units lost fewer men to enemy resistance than to a "point system" adopted after the end of the European conflict. Based on elaborate calculations of total service, overseas duty, days in combat, and wounds, eligible men were sent home once they had accumulated eighty-five points. Although the 38th stood to lose fewer key men than some veteran outfits, the point system would have exempted many of the division's original Kentucky and Indiana guardsmen from participation in the invasion of Japan. "I do not suppose there is an army in the history of the world that discharged its veterans just before a big battle," fretted Lt. Gen. Robert L. Eichelberger, whose Eighth Army assumed control of Luzon on July 1.

Mercifully, the likely fierceness of a March 1946 Battle of Tokyo was to remain a moot point, but there was no doubt that the Japanese surrendering themselves in the Philippines were in wretched condition. At first, only a trickle of individuals came out of hiding, each carrying a bamboo stick to which was tied a tiny bag of rice. Sternly, Arthur Bonneycastle, who had transferred to the 6th Division, forbade his men from taking potshots at Japanese trying to surrender. Later on larger groups came in, among them individuals anxious to trade "fountain pens that wouldn't write" for American cigarrettes. It was hard to realize that such pathetic characters had so recently been the scourge of the Far East.

Infinitely distressing to American eyes were the long-imprisoned 1941-42 defenders of Bataan, some of whom were liberated in the Philippines. Many others were still closely guarded in Japan itself. By 1945 only thirty-seven of the original sixty-six Harrodsburg, Kentucky, National Guard tankers were still alive. From a prison camp in northern Japan Captain Edwin Rue tried to follow the unfolding course of the war. Like all of the Americans surrendered on 9 April 1942, Rue had been undernourished and exhausted when taken into captivity. On the infamous five-day Death March sixty miles north from Bataan to Camp O'Donnell, he was fed only a little rice. His thirst he simply endured; others who downed brackish water from carabao tracks later died "like flies." Rue did not personally witness Japanese guards shooting or bayoneting prisoners during the march, but he did see men "taken off to the bushes" from which they did not return. Inevitably, there were opportunities for escape from the serpentine column of thousands of prisoners, but Rue decided against it. On alien Luzon he could think of "no place for a white man to hide."

Rue would have died of beriberi before leaving the Philippines had not Yandell Terhune of Harrodsburg provided him with vitamin pills. An enlisted man frequently sent out on work details, Terhune somehow obtained the precious tablets. Fortunately, Rue was among the captives transferred to Japan before American submarines and planes turned the voyage north from the Philippines into a suicidal gauntlet. Many Americans aboard Japanese cattle-boats were inadvertently killed by their own countrymen. In one convoy to Japan John Sadler of Harrodsburg watched the destruction of an oil tanker, wondering anxiously if his ship was to be torpedoed next. Surviving the perilous journey, Sadler was put to work in an undersea coal mine near Nagasaki. At Osaka, Edwin Rue watched fully a third of those confined with him in a warehouse die during their first Japanese winter. At his next camp, a mountainside compound for Allied officers, conditions were somewhat better. The prisoners established a senior committee to maintain discipline and bargain with the camp authorities.

By 1945 Rue and his compatriots could hear the overhead roar of hundreds of B-29 Superfortresses coming to ignite with incendiary bombs the highly flammable, jerry-built cities of Japan. Then in August 1945 Rue learned from camp guards that the "Yankee vultures" had dropped a terrible new bomb on Hiroshima. Overnight, the profound shock of the atomic bomb stripped the Japanese of their former arrogance. A second American nuclear device was exploded on August 9 over Nagasaki, where the blast was witnessed by John Sadler who happened to be in the messhall of his prison camp at the moment of detonation: "They dropped that bomb, and at first we thought it was a earthquake. But she come with such a roar, and the . . . building swung way over like a forty-degree angle. . . . We . . . saw an awful toadstool just across the bay, and it towered up there, I guess 4,500 feet high." Several days later Sadler inspected the site of the blast: "Nagasaki was just like . . . [a] highway. Everything was . . . level. . . . You could pick up a rock in your bare hand and just crumble it to powder. And Pullman cars was laying five and six blocks from the railroad tracks. . . . It was a tremendous heat. And there . . . [were] people sitting . . . [whose] carcass[es] . . . never had fallen over, with all the meat gone."

Japan surrendered just six days after the Nagasaki bomb. Several weeks were yet to pass before all of the Americans in enemy hands were recovered. With unloaded weapons Japanese prison-camp guards remained at their posts—to protect the inmates. From Edwin Rue's remote camp the West Pointer William A. Orr made his way to Kyoto, where he managed to report the whereabouts of the 350 captives. Early on September 10—eight days after General MacArthur received the surrender of Japan at a ceremony aboard a battleship in Tokyo Bay—six B-29s shook the compound as they thundered over at just 350 feet. From their open bomb-bays dropped parachutes (of various colors) with suspended fifty-five-gallon drums packed with food, medicine, bedding, and magazines. Later, doctors and nurses arrived by truck from Kyoto to minister to the inmates of the almost-forgotten camp.

With other released prisoners Edwin Rue was evacuated to Manila, where he saw a familiar emblem: the cyclone patch of the 8th Division. But he did not encounter any of the men with whom he had entered federal service so very long ago. Somehow it did not much matter. The time had come to make a new beginning to life.

Epilogue

O N 2 SEPTEMBER 1945, as civilization ended its most titanic war, General MacArthur accepted the surrender of the Japanese Empire on the deck of the U.S.S. *Missouri*. The dawning of the nuclear age, MacArthur somberly acknowledged, had revised "the traditional concepts of war. . . . We have had our last chance. If we do not now devise some greater and more equitable system, Armageddon will be at our door." Most of the Kentuckians reentering civilian life in 1945-46 had not yet cast their thoughts so far ahead. Whatever nuclear weapons might portend for future generations, men returning from the Pacific sensed that the atomic bombs of 1945 had spared them the ordeal of invading Japan. Whether in fact the invasion would otherwise have been necessary remains uncertain.

Hardened for the most part by a rural heritage and by the Great Depression of the 1930s, the Kentucky fighting men of 1941-45 differed rather less from their predecessors of 1861-65 than might have been anticipated. If they were not especially eager to serve, few Americans of the 1940s questioned traditional patriotic verities or the necessity of seeing the conflict through to victory. In World War II Kentucky had produced its share of heroes—and victims of battle fatigue. Most fighting men from the Bluegrass State were neither paladins nor psychoneurotic cases; they were average people enduring a sometimes dangerous, and often extremely boring, experience. In 1945 most could take some satisfaction from well-performed services, hazardous and routine alike. The strengths and weaknesses of Kentuckians in World War II were those of most American combatants. Only as infantrymen had the Americans of 1941-45 failed to win the highest accolades of both allies and foes, a phenomenon for which the nation's mobilization practices and machine-oriented society furnished persuasive explanations. Moreover, not until 1944 had more than a comparatively few American troops engaged in extended ground combat. Not until 1945 did they generally match in experience the soldiers of other countries. If the American soldier of 1941-45 did not surpass the German in tactical skill, the Russian in endurance, the Britisher in defensive doggedness, or the Japanese in fanatical self-sacrifice, he nevertheless won his battles.

Kentuckians returning from the war could anticipate successful personal futures. Generous educational benefits and a high overall level of national prosperity during the 1950s and 1960s meant that the average World War II veteran would fare better materially than his forefathers. Some Kentuckians sought postwar military careers. A few were to bear the military responsibility for the life or death of the nation. Russell E. Dougherty would head the Air Force's Strategic Air Command in the 1970s. Charles K. Duncan would command the Atlantic Fleet as a full admiral before his retirement in 1972. Kenneth M. Carr (the one time enlisted sailor in the Solomon Islands) would command as a vice-admiral the submarines of the Atlantic Fleet in the late 1970s.

Between 1950 and 1973 Kentuckians were to take a full part in two large-scale, but "limited," wars. William E. Barber was to win the Medal of Honor in Korea, a distinction coming to five Kentuckians in that conflict and five more in Vietnam. Like others pondering America's costly failure in Vietnam, where he participated in his third war, Barber observes that the fighting men there seemed to be a "different breed" from their World War II predecessors. But Barber is quick to emphasize that "the combat actions (and values, attitudes, courage) involved with the V[iet] N[am] War will compare favorably with those of any war in our nation's history." It should be noted that in racial proportions the American combatants of Vietnam were indeed significantly unlike their predecessors of 1941-45. Only after the issuance of a 1948 presidential executive order were blacks integrated with whites in the American armed forces.

In the second half of the twentieth century American fighting men confronted a strategic and moral dilemma that had not constrained earlier generations. The very destructiveness of the weapons in the American and Soviet arsenals of the last three decades posed a continuing threat to the future of civilization itself. In both Korea and Vietnam the unrestrained pursuit of victory would have entailed an intolerable level of risk for the United States. In neither conflict had the nation been dismembered, or even directly attacked as in 1861, 1917, or 1941. Nor was the military purpose of Korea and Vietnam the outright destruction of such tangible evils as slavery or Nazi totalitarianism. The highest strategically feasible military goal of both conflicts was the mere restoration of the prewar status quo. Surely, these realities affected the outlook, attitude, and morale of Americans in Korea and Vietnam. Nothing has transpired since 1945 to indicate that anything on the order of the three great national military crusades of the previous eighty-four years can ever recur.

Acknowledgments and Sources

THIS BOOK owes much to many individuals and several institutions. My investigations were facilitated by a grant from the faculty research committee of Western Kentucky University and by special-assignment release time for which I am indebted to Richard L. Troutman, head of the history department. My faculty colleagues Lowell H. Harrison, Marion B. Lucas, and Nancy D. Baird have read and commented upon all or parts of the manuscript, as have Thomas D. and Elizabeth Turner Clark of Lexington, Kentucky. Walter L. Hixson supplied information about Richard E. Bush on Okinawa.

I received valuable assistance from the following libraries and librarians: the Kentucky Library at Western Kentucky University, Elaine Harrison and Patricia Hodges; the Special Collections at the University of Kentucky Library, William Marshall and Claire McCann; the Kentucky Military History Museum at Frankfort, Nickey Hughes; the Filson Club, James Bentley; and the Archives and Records Center at the University of Louisville, Sherrill McConnell and Thomas Owen. I also spent some profitable hours in the clipping file at the Louisville Free Public Library. Most of all, my wife Elizabeth and daughter Marye have rendered possible the completion of this study by their continuing interest in it and their patience with the author. In no way are any of the persons or institutions mentioned above responsible for shortcomings in the manuscript.

An annotated copy of this work has been deposited in the Kentucky Library for use by readers wishing to check specific source references.

Based as it is upon primary materials the foregoing text reflects the differing types of sources used in covering different eras. The Civil War is richer than the wars of our own century in available collections of letters. Undoubtedly, many valuable manuscripts of twentieth-century conflicts will in the future find their way into archival collections. Whether they will match in interest the documents of the Civil War remains uncertain, because the severe censorship of the 1917-18 and 1941-45 wars cramped the writing styles of many participants. Moreover, men of our century often have had less time to compose lengthy epistles than had their grandfathers of the 1860s. Our age is also more habituated to verbal than to written personal communication. If the prose of the 1860s was florid, it was nevertheless a style that cultivated descriptive talent.

Fortunately for me, oral history can be used for the investigation of World War II. While it is true that men in their fifties, sixties, and seventies tend to have selective memories of events that took place some four decades ago, they still remember many things. Even interviews that may have seemed unproductive when taped have often furnished valuable insights.

Whatever the sources of participants' descriptions of American wars, I have sought where possible to let eyewitnesses speak for themselves. For the sake of clarity, I have felt free when quoting written materials to alter initial capitalization and terminal punctuation. I have, however, reproduced all internal capitalization and spelling as it appears in the original documents.

The following sources were the principal ones used in treating the Civil War. In the Special Collections at the University of Kentucky: the T. Robert McBeath Papers; the B.F. Buckner Collection; the Herndon Family Papers; the Means Family Collection; the Gunn Collection; a letter of Milton B. Cox to his wife, dated 9 October 1862; the Diary of Hubbard Milward; the Fackler Family Papers; a letter of Jeremiah T. Boyle to Don Carlos Buell, dated 5 January 1862; Robert T. Bean, "Seventeen Months a Prisoner in Camp Douglas," which is the transcript of a paper apparently published in *The Confederate Veteran* early in the twentieth century; Robert T. Bean, "Then and Now," a typescript dated October 1912; and letters from W.H. Cundiff to J.T. Cundiff, dated 8 and 11 November 1864. In the Kentucky Library at Western Kentucky University: the Lewis-Starling Collection; and a typed copy of a letter from A.W. Randolph to his parents, dated 27 September 1863. In the Filson Club: the Thomas Speed Letterbook; and the Stone Family Papers and Diary of J.D. Sprake, both of which are typed copies of items held by the Kentucky Historical Society in Frankfort. Two particularly useful secondary works are Lowell H. Harrison, *The Civil War in Kentucky* (Lexington, Ky., 1975); and William C. Davis, *The Orphan Brigade: The Kentucky Confederates Who Couldn't Go Home* (Garden City, N.Y., 1980).

On the emergence of a modern American military establishment I have made use of the following. In the Filson Club: a manuscript life of James Edward Jouett written by Alfred Pirtle and kept with the Pirtle

Collection; and the Todd Family Papers, Correspondence, 1870-89. In the Kentucky Library the Green Collection, which includes letters by S.I.M. Major. In the Special Collections of the University of Kentucky "Reminisences," a carbon copy of a lengthy memoir by George B. Duncan which covers the early part of his career and is kept with the Wilson Collection. Among published primary and secondary works are Hugh Rodman, *Yarns of a Kentucky Admiral* (Indianapolis, 1928); Heath Twichell, Jr., *Allen: The Biography of an Army Officer, 1859-1930* (New Brunswick, N.J., 1975), which was also useful on the First World War; and Edgar Frank Raines, Jr., "Major General J. Franklin Bell and Military Reform: The Chief of Staff Years, 1906-1910" (Ph.D. diss., University of Wisconsin, 1976).

On World War I, I have depended upon these materials. In the Special Collections at the University of Kentucky: the immense Wilson Collection, which includes correspondence to and from Samuel Wilson, along with George B. Duncan's typescript memoir, "Reminiscences of the World War," as well as assorted clippings on a variety of war topics; the Felix C. Holt Collection; the Howard Kinne Papers; and the Barrow Unit box in which are kept assorted clippings and memorabilia. In the Kentucky Library the Victor H. Strahm Collection. In the Kentucky Historical Society the Diary of Austin Kinniard. In the University of Louisville's Archives and Records Center the Diary of Michael A. Lewis. By far the best book on its subject is Edward M. Coffman, *The War to End All Wars: The American Military Experience in World War I* (New York, 1968). An extremely interesting work that combines history with personal reminiscence is Laurence Stallings, *The Doughboys: The Story of the AEF, 1917-1918* (New York, 1963), upon which I depended for information about Samuel Woodfill.

On Kentuckians in World War II, my greatest single debt is to Harry L. Jackson of Bowling Green who made available to me his personal letters from the European Theater of Operations. Mr. Jackson has subsequently deposited these documents in the Kentucky Library. Adding interest to the letters are numerous drawings and sketches that he made during the war. John Elmore Sadler dictated in 1961 his account of his experiences in the Philippines and in captivity; the transcript is held by the Kentucky Historical Society. Two published memoirs by Kentuckians are Philip Ardery, *Bomber Pilot: A Memoir of World War II* (Lexington, Ky., 1978), the first draft of which was composed shortly after the author's return from the war and while the events described were still fresh in his memory; and Janice Holt Giles, ed., *The G.I. Journal of Sergeant Giles* (Boston, 1965). A contemporary account of Creed Burlingame's submarine is Robert Trumbell, *Silversides* (New York, 1945).

Husband E. Kimmel's apologia is *Admiral Kimmel's Story* (Chicago, 1955). Others discussing the Pearl Harbor disaster are Lloyd J. Graybar, "Pearl Harbor 'Scapegoat,' " *Louisville Courier-Journal Magazine* (3 December 1978); and Martin V. Melosi, *The Shadow of Pearl Harbor: Political Controversy Over the Surprise Attack, 1941-1946* (College Station, Texas, 1978). Simon B. Buckner, Jr., was the subject of a *Time* cover story on 16 June 1945. His career is also detailed in various newspaper accounts and general histories of the war in the Pacific. Willis A. Lee's activities are discussed in naval histories of the Pacific operations, notably by Samuel Eliot Morison, *The Struggle for Guadalcanal, August 1942-February 1943* (Boston, 1949), and *Leyte, June 1944-January 1945* (Boston, 1958). On the liberation of the Philippines, the 38th Division put together a picture album for its members. It resembles a college annual in format. I am indebted to Ray Cossey, a member of the division during the Luzon campaign, for lending me his copy. William C. Chase published his recollections some three decades after leading the Avengers of Bataan on Luzon. His memoir is entitled *Front Line General: The Commands of William C. Chase, An Autobiography* (Houston, Texas, 1975). I interviewed the following men about their experiences in World War II: William E. Barber, Arthur C. Bonneycastle, William R. Buster, Creed C. Burlingame, Kenneth M. Carr, Harry Caudill, Lowell H. Harrison, Walter W. Hillenmeyer, Jr., Robert F. Houlihan, Laban P. Jackson, William J. Marshall, Chester Mercer, John D. Minton, Edwin W. Rue, and Weldon P. Shouse. Also granting me interviews on the post-1945 period were Robert A. Carraco, Russell E. Dougherty, Gary A. Riggs, Harry G. Thomas, and Jerry Ward. Finally, several individuals have written or called to make suggestions or to furnish helpful leads, a few of which, I regret to say, I was unable to follow up. However, my greatest regret is that my friend Chester Mercer did not live to see this volume in print.

Index

Ainsworth, Fred, 39
Alexander, Harold, 72, 73, 77
Alger, Russell A., 38
Allen, Henry T., 30, 35, 37-38, 39, 46, 54-55
Allen, Terry, 81
Ancon, 81
Anderson, Robert, 1
Andersonville, 22
Annapolis, 27, 29, 30, 97
Annapolis, 33
Anzio, 71-72
Appomattox, 23
Ardery, Philip, 80
Argonne Forest, 46-47, 55-56
Armistice (World War I), 40, 53
Army Specialized Training Program, 66
Atlanta, campaign of, 9, 15, 19, 23
Atlantic, battle of, 66-68
Atomic bomb, 114
Attu, 104

Baker, Newton D., 40-41
Banks, James, 3
Barber, William E., 65, 102-4, 117
Barrow, David, 54
Bataan: Death March, 113; fall of, 61-63, 113; liberation of, 108-9
Bean, Robert T., 22, 23-24
Bell, J. Franklin, 31, 35, 36-37, 38-39, 46
Bonneycastle, Arthur C., 107-8, 109, 111, 113
Boyle, Jeremiah T., 17
Bradley, Omar N., 69, 81
Bragg, Braxton, 2, 4, 25
Brandy Station, Va., 21
Breckinridge, John C., 12, 24

Brereton, Lewis H., 60
Bristow, Benjamin H., 8, 10-11
Brown, Joe E., 112
Bruce, Sanders, 18
Buchenwald prison camp, 90-91
Buckner, Benjamin F., 2, 4-5, 8-10, 18
Buckner, Simon B., Jr., 104-7
Buell, Don Carlos, 4, 17
Buford, John, 20-21
Bulge, Battle of the, 86-88
Bull Run, Second, 20
Burlingame, Creed C., 97-99
Bush, Richard E., 106
Buster, William R., 66, 84-85, 89

Camp Croft, 65
Camp Douglas, 21-22
Camp Kearney, 43
Camp O'Donnell, 113
Camp Shelby, 59, 64
Camp Taylor, 41
Carr, Kenneth M., 99, 117
Caudill, Harry, 65, 66, 68, 69, 73-76
Chase, William C., 108-9, 112
Chiang Kai-shek, 29
Chickamauga, Tenn., 12, 46
Civil War, Confederate units in: Army of Northern Virginia, 19; Army of Tennessee, 24; Orphan Brigade, 12, 25; 8th Kentucky Cavalry, 7, 21, 22; 9th Kentucky Cavalry, 3
Civil War, Union units in: Army of the Ohio, 4; Army of the Tennessee, 19; XIV Corps, 12; Louisville Legion, 25; 2d Kentucky, 10; 14th Kentucky, 5, 13, 17; 18th Kentucky, 9; 20th Kentucky, 4,

123

Civil War, Union units in (*cont.*)
18; 21st Kentucky, 6; 27th
Kentucky, 2; 8th Kentucky
Cavalry, 8
Clark, Mark W., 70, 72, 73, 77
Clark Field, 60
Clemenceau, Georges, 44
Combined Bomber Offensive, 78-79
Command and General Staff School, 39
Cox, Milton B., 7
Crittenden, John J., 26
Crowder, Enoch, 42
Cundiff, W.H., 23

Davis, Jefferson, 19, 24
Dawes, B.F., 41
D Day, 81, 82
Dewey, George, 33-34
Dickman, Joseph T., 54
Donovan, Herman L., 59
Dougherty, Russell E., 117
Draft (military conscription), 2, 3, 40-41, 63-65
Duncan, Charles K., 117
Duncan, George B., 31, 32, 35, 36, 39, 44, 46, 48-49

Easley, Roy W., 108
Eichelberger, Robert L., 112
Eisenhower, Dwight D., 68, 85, 86, 89, 93
Emancipation Proclamation, 10
Empress of Japan, 68

Fackler, C.W., 11
Fort Benjamin Harrison, 42
Fort Donelson, 19
Fort Hayes, 66
Fort Henry, 19
Fort Knox, 59, 65
Fort Leavenworth, 39
Fort Sheridan, 32
Fort Stotsenberg, 60
Fort Sumter, 1
Fort Wingate, 31
Foster, Paul, 91
Franklin, Tenn., 19

Garfield, James A., 13-14, 18
Gettysburg, Pa., 21

Giles, Henry, 89
Grant, Ulysses S., 19
Gray, Horace M., 44, 45
Gruenther, Alfred M., 70
Guadalcanal, Second, 94-95, 97
Gunn, Thomas, 6, 11

Haggin, Louis, 54
Halleck, Henry W., 7
Halsey, William F., Jr., 95-96, 105
Harbison, Clinton, 42
Harrison, Lowell H., 65, 66, 67, 86, 90, 92, 93
Hartford, 29
Helm, Ben Hardin, 12
Herndon, Richard, 2
Hillenmeyer, Walter W., Jr., 69, 81-82, 87
Hodges, Courtney H., 87
Holt, Felix C., 43-44, 56
Home Guards, 3
Hood, John Bell, 19-20
Houlihan, Robert F., 77-79
Huebner, Clarence R., 69, 80-82

Indian wars: 9th Regiment in, 31; 7th Cavalry in, 31
Influenza epidemic (1918), 47
Island No. 10, battle of, 20
Italy, campaign of, 69-77
Iwo Jima, 101-4, 110; flag raising, 102

Jackson, Harry L., 65, 82, 85-86, 90-91
Jackson, James S., 2, 15-16
Jackson, Laban P., 69, 70, 76-77
Johnson, Andrew, 24
Johnston, Albert Sidney, 19-20
Johnston, Joseph E., 24
Joint Chiefs of Staff, 100, 107
Jones, H.L.C., 108
Jouett, James E., 26-27
Jouett, Matthew, 26

Kesselring, Field Marshal, 76
Kimmel, Husband E., 57-58, 60
King, Ernest J., 29, 94, 106
Kinkaid, Thomas C., 96
Kinne, Howard, 43, 52-53
Kinniard, Austin, 55

Kirishima, 95
Korean War, 117-18
Kurita, Admiral, 96

Lagrew, Embry D., 83-84, 90, 91, 92
Lawrence, David, 106
Lee, R.E., 19, 20, 23, 24
Lee, Willis A., Jr., 94-97
Lewis, Michael A., 41, 47, 53
Leyte Gulf, 96
Lincoln, Abraham, 10, 23
Longstreet, James, 12
Lucas, John P., 72
Luzon, 59-63, 107-13

MacArthur, Arthur, 37
MacArthur, Douglas, 60, 61, 62, 63, 96, 114, 116
McBeath, T. Robert, 2, 6-7, 9
McClellan, George B., 20
McCormack, John, 54
McKinley, William, 32, 34, 36-37
Magic (decoder), 58
Mahan, Alfred T., 29
Major, S.I.M., 28-29, 32-33
Manila Bay, battle of, 33-34
Marine Corps, U.S., 64, 65, 100-104, 105, 106
Marshall, George C., 68
Marshall, Humphrey, 14
Marshall, William J., 29, 67, 80
Maynard brothers, 110
Means, Arch, 5, 7, 13-15, 17-18
Medal of Honor, 36, 106, 117
Mercer, Chester, 67, 82-83, 88, 89
Merritt, Wesley, 36
Metacomet, 27
Middle Creek, Ky., 13
Midway Islands, 94
Miles, Nelson A., 38
Milward, Hubbard, 9, 23
Minton, John D., 65, 100-101
Mitscher, Marc A., 95-96
Mobile Bay, 27
Mobilization: in World War I, 40-41; in World War II, 57, 63-66
Monte Cassino, 71-72
Moore, Laban T., 17-18
Morgan, John Hunt, 6, 20; "Big Raid" of, 20
Morison, Samuel Eliot, 95

Morris, Mary Blackburn, 22
Murray, E.H., 11

Nagasaki, 114
Nagumo, Admiral, 57
Nashville, Tenn., 19
National Guard, 40, 41, 46, 59, 107, 108, 113
Naval War College, 29
Navy Department, 58
New York, 33
Nimitz, Chester W., 105, 106
Normandy, 69, 71, 77, 79, 80-83
Nuremberg trials, 91

Office of Strategic Services (OSS), 77-79
Okinawa, 104-7
Olympia, 34
Omaha Beach, 80-81
Operation Diadem, 76
Operation Overlord, 77
Orr, William A., 114

Patton, George S., Jr., 68-69, 77, 87
Pearl Harbor, 57-58, 59, 60
Peleliu, 100-101, 110
Perguson, D. Carl, Jr., 66
Perryville, Ky., 7, 15-16, 18, 56
Pershing, John J., 45, 46, 50, 54, 56
Philippine Commission, 37
Philippine Constabulary, 37
Philippine Insurrection, 34-38; U.S. 4th Regiment in, 35, 36
Point system (World War II demobilization), 112
Pope, John, 20, 21
Prisons, Civil War, 21, 22

Raleigh, 34
Randolph, A.W., 12
Reese, Harold "Pee Wee," 87
Remagen Bridge, 88-89
Richardson, Robert C., Jr., 105
Rodman, Hugh, 29-30, 33-34
Rome, liberation of, 74-77
Roosevelt, Franklin D., 58, 59, 66, 78, 95
Roosevelt, Theodore, 33, 35, 40
Root, Elihu, 38
Rosecrans, William S., 11, 12

Rousseau, Lovell H., 18
Rue, Edwin W., 59-63, 113-15

Sadler, John E., 61-62, 113-14
Saint Mihiel, 46
Salerno, 69-70
Sandlin, Willie, 49, 50
Schofield, John M., 31
Scott, Hugh L., 31, 40
Selma, 27
Shannon, Jasper, 59
Sharp, Dr., 21
Sherman, William T., 11, 15, 23, 24
Shiloh, Tenn., 18, 19, 46
Short, Walter C., 57, 58
Shouse, Weldon P., 65, 69, 70-71, 76
Sicily, campaign of, 81
Silversides, 97-99
Simpson, William H., 85
Smith, E. Kirby, 25
Smith, Holland M., 105
Smith, Ralph, 105
Sousley, Franklin R., 102
South Dakota, 94-95
Soviet Army, 89, 92
Spanish-American War, 32-34; 4th Regiment in, 32
Speed, Thomas, 5, 15
Sprake, J.D., 7-8, 21, 22-23
Spruance, Raymond A., 95-96, 105-6
Starling, Samuel M., 2, 4, 6, 9-11, 15-16
State Department, 58
Stimson, Henry L., 39
Stone, Henry Lane, 3, 8, 21-22, 24, 25
Stone, Valentine H., 25
Stone's River, Tenn., 11
Strahm, Victor H., 43, 50-52
Surrender of Germany (V-E Day), 87, 89-90, 93
Surrender of Japan (V-J Day), 114, 116

Taft, William Howard, 37, 39
Terhune, Yandell, 113
Todd, Chapman C., 27-28
Townsend, James, 88
Tracy, 80

Truscott, Lucian K., Jr., 72
Turner, Richmond Kelly, 95

United Services Organization (USO), 112
United States Military Academy (West Point), 17, 27, 30, 31, 84, 114
United States Naval Academy (Annapolis), 27, 29, 30, 97
Units, military. *See name of conflict*
University of Kentucky, 42, 52, 59, 65

Vandegrift, A.A., 106
Victory Program, 63-64
Vietnam War, 35, 117-18

Wainwright, Jonathan M., 60, 62-63
War Department, 3, 38, 41, 42, 58, 64, 107
Washington, 94-95
Wawa Dam, 111
Weaver, James R.N., 60
Western Kentucky University, 51
Western Task Force, 66, 67
West Point, 17, 27, 30, 31, 84, 114
Williams, D.R., 47
Wilson, Henry Maitland, 73
Wilson, Samuel M., 42, 44
Wilson, Woodrow, 40, 56
Winslow, 67
Wood, Leonard, 33, 39, 40
Woodfill, Samuel, 49-50
World War I, 39-56; U.S. military units in: First Army, 46; American Expeditionary Force, 50, 53; Base Hospital No. 40, 54; Services of Supply, 53; 115th Field Signal Battalion, 43; 164th Brigade, 49; 1st Division, 44; 5th Division, 49; 38th Division, 46; 77th Division, 39, 42, 46, 49; 82d Division, 46, 48-49; 84th Division, 46; 90th Division, 46; 26th Regiment, 44; 91st Aero Squadron, 51; 99th Aero Squadron, 53
World War II, U.S. military units in: First Army, 86, 87, 88, 89; Third Army, 87; Fifth Army, 69, 70, 72; Sixth Army, 106; Seventh

www.ingramcontent.com/pod-product-compliance
Lightning Source LLC
Chambersburg PA
CBHW032052150426
43194CB00006B/507